WOMAN LOVE YOUR BODY

(And Let Your Husband Love It Too!)

Apostle Louis S. Greenup, Jr.
"The Marriage Doctor"

WOMAN LOVE YOUR BODY
(And Let Your Husband Love It Too!)

ISBN #1-885342-07-1   United States $22.95   Canada $24.95

Copyrighted © 1995 by Louis S. Greenup, Jr.
Covenant Winners Network
P.O. Box 52827
Baton Rouge, Louisiana 70805

Published by
Creative Ways
509 Marie Drive
South Holland, Illinois 60473

Library of Congress Cataloging in Publication Data
Greenup, Louis S.
Woman Love Your Body (And Let Your Husband Love It Too!)
by Louis S. Greenup, Jr.
ISBN 1-885342-07-1
I. Title - Revised Edition
96-96285

All Scriptures are derived from the King James version of the Bible unless otherwise indicated. Printed in the United States of America.

WOMAN LOVE YOUR BODY

(And Let Your Husband Love It Too!)

Apostle Louis S. Greenup, Jr.
"The Marriage Doctor"

A Creative Ways Publication

"...she shall be called Woman..."

Genesis 2:23

DEDICATION

This book is dedicated to Karen, my wife, the first lady of love in my life. To my princess, my queen, my mistress and my *"Good Thing!"*

L.O.U.I.S. Song
(<u>L</u>oving <u>O</u>nly <u>U</u> <u>I</u>s <u>S</u>weet)

I've got a Good Thing at home;
My mind don't need to roam;
I've got a Good Thing at home;
My mind don't need to roam;
I've got a Good Thing at home;
My mind don't need to roam.

I've got a good, good, good,
I've got a Good Thing at home.
Yeah, Yeah!

With the Lord up above,
And the wife that I love,
The other woman is out the door,
I don't need her anymore!

I've got a good, good, good,
I've got a Good Thing at home.

With Christ in my heart,
My love for you will never part;
I've got a brand new life,
And a beautiful, lovely wife!

I've got a good, good, good,
I've got a Good Thing at home.
Thank God!

A HOLY GHOST HIT FROM HEAVEN

#1 On the Chart of Your Husband's Heart,
A Love Song Guaranteed to Make Your Marriage Strong,
If You Sing It All the Day Long.
A Love Story for God's Glory.

Proverbs 18:22

ACKNOWLEDGMENTS

From its inception, this revised handbook has had the support, prayers and advice of so many people that I could not possibly acknowledge them all. Nevertheless, I will take the time to recognize just a few of them.

First, to the three most important people in my life; my beautiful wife Karen and my two sons Josiah and Daniel. Thank you for your patience, endurance and love. Your support means everything to me. I thank God for you.

Second, to my administrator Joyce Williams; for her hours of research, the labor she spent pulling my thoughts together to form this book and for going the extra mile.

Third, to my mother Betty Greenup; thank you for sharing your wisdom. Your insight on exercise and dieting will help women everywhere learn to cherish and preserve their bodies.

And last but certainly not least, I want to thank the members of my church–Christ the Deliverer Assembly. Your prayers and support made this book possible. I want each member to know that Karen and I love and appreciate you very much.

Apostle Louis S. Greenup, Jr.

ABOUT THE AUTHOR

Apostle Louis Smith Greenup, Jr. is the founder and president of Christ the Deliverer Assembly in Baton Rouge, Louisiana. He and his wife Karen, reside with their two sons Josiah and Daniel at Greenup Estates, home of "The Shepherd's Inn Program."

As a philosophy student at Southern University in Baton Rouge, Louis Greenup became interested in the human body and how it works. Taking pre-med courses was the first step in his quest to understand God's awesome creation–the body. His aspiration to become a medical doctor was transformed into reality many years later through ministry.

While in college, Louis Greenup was well on his way to a career as a professional baseball pitcher when a personal crisis brought him to a crossroads in his life. He was forced to make a decision regarding God, chose to follow Jesus Christ and has never regretted it. As the name of his ministry implies, Apostle Greenup proclaims that CHRIST is the Deliverer—not a man or a church. Only the Lord Jesus can set the human spirit, soul and body free.

Apostle Greenup has traveled extensively throughout the United States for the past 20 years. The call of God upon his life has taken him to South America, the Virgin Islands, Puerto Rico, Guyana, Mexico and the Bahamas. Through his anointed preaching and unique teaching ministry, millions of people have been touched, saved, healed and delivered. His candid, practical and humorous approach to ministry has wrought deliverance to all types and races. Two intricate parts of Apostle Greenup's worldwide outreach are the "Weekend For Winners" and "Singles That Win" seminars.

Affectionately known as *"The Marriage Doctor,"* Apostle Greenup teaches married couples how to love better, stronger and longer. "Singles That Win" focuses on teenagers, divorcees, widows, and singles alike. The seminars address such issues as marriage preparation and preservation. Singles are taught how to have "victory in their virginity" and how to prepare for marriage spiritually, emotionally, mentally and physically. Apostle Greenup's song "No Wed No Bed" has become the rallying cry for teens, singles and young adults across the nation.

FOREWORD

Through our years of ministry and counseling with women, we have found that most women are not happy with their bodies. As a whole, women live in constant fear of whether their bodies measure up to the world's standard of the "perfect body image." The Bible tells us in 1 John 4:18, *"There is no fear in love; but perfect love casteth out fear...."* This is the concept that my husband emphasizes in Woman Love Your Body. When women acquire knowledge and understanding of their bodies, they will no longer accept the deceptions and lies that today's society imposes upon them. They will see themselves as the unique and marvelous creations that God has made them. With acceptance and in appreciation, women all over the earth will truly love their bodies.

The Bible declares in 1 Corinthians 13:4-8, *"Love suffereth long, and is kind; love envieth not; love vaunteth not itself, is not puffed up, Doth not behave itself unseemly, seeketh not her own, is not easily provoked, thinketh no evil; Rejoiceth not in iniquity, but rejoiceth in the truth; Beareth all things, believeth all things, hopeth all things, endureth all things. Love never faileth...the greatest of these is love."* This is the kind of love that God wants women to have for their bodies. He wants us to joyfully endure all of the changes our bodies go through and still be patient and kind to our bodies.

Woman Love Your Body is the result of years of intense research and study by Apostle Greenup. This revised handbook is designed to help women of all ages, sizes and shapes develop a positive self-image of their bodies through biblical principles, anatomical information and the practical applications that are defined in this book.

The style of writing is characteristic of my husband's preaching—graphic, yet amusing and motivating. This handbook possesses a wealth of information that is not only educational but also inspirational.

In Chapter One, "From Head to Toe, Love Must Flow," women are taught the power of the tongue in relationship to developing a positive self-image of their bodies through the five kinds of "love": agape, phileo, storge, epithumia and eros.

In Chapter Three, "A 'B.A.' Degree Concerning My Anatomy," women receive general knowledge of their bodies and its functions. This consists of the nine body systems, common health problems, self-exams (genital and breast), feminine hygiene, personal care, nutrition and exercise. After studying this chapter, every woman can confidently say that she has a basic understanding of her anatomy.

In Chapter Six, "Sexhersize," the concept and term "Sexhersize" is explained.

"Sexhersize" is the education and knowledge of female sexuality regardless of your body size, style and shape. The "Sexhersize" activities are a wonderful addition to any woman's repertoire of personal care and pampering.

In Chapter Seven, Apostle Greenup offers what he considers the best six doctors to help maintain the youth, strength and health of the female body. These "love doctors" are air, water, light, exercise, massage and lubrication.

The affirmations, facts and innovative sayings in Woman Love Your Body will encourage and motivate women of all ages to "love" their bodies. This will strengthen their individual self-worth and add to the fibre of love in their marriage.

I thank God for my husband's diligence to write this book. Woman Love Your Body has been a tremendous blessing to me and my life. I appreciate and love my body more than I ever did in the past. In addition, I am absolutely thrilled to present and give my body to my husband. Even though this book was written specifically for women, men should read it too! I pray that this handbook encourages husbands and men of God to study their wife's body and help their spouse cultivate a love for their physiques.

Every husband should be knowledgeable about his wife's body, understand her feelings about it and protect her from fears, doubts, diseases, infections and unnecessary surgeries. In doing so, every man will be the priest and protector of his wife as God originally intended him to be. It is my desire that with the proper and continual use of this handbook, every husband will have a confident, self-assured, sensual wife. Glory to God!

I charge all women to take the title of this book as if it was God's law and decree to follow. "Woman Love Your Body!"

In closing, Job 22:28 says, "Thou shalt also decree a thing, and it shall be established unto thee...." The Word of the Lord to womenkind everywhere is: Love your body! Celebrate your femininity! Enjoy your sensuality! And cherish what God has made you—a beautiful WOMAN!

Mrs. Karen H. Greenup

TABLE OF CONTENTS

INTRODUCTION

This handbook is written for women, especially wives, who hate their shapes, detest their sizes, abhor their figures and despise their thighs. It is written for every woman who feels fat, forgotten, frustrated and frigid. It is written for the wives who feel oversized and undersexed, old and cold, neglected and rejected, bored and ignored and rigid and frigid. And it is written for women who cannot relax to enjoy climax and have no enthusiasm for orgasm.

This book was also written to minister to women who have experienced emotional or sexual trauma. For example, if you are the victim of rape or incest; if you've had a hysterectomy, a mastectomy or an abortion; or if you are anorexic or bulimic this handbook is for you. You may ask yourself, "How can this book help me?" I've discovered that many women who have experienced any of the above are scarred and have negative self-images. Because of these trials, some women even hate their bodies. The solution is to acknowledge the hurt, release it, forgive yourself and love your body.

Women across America and around the world are constantly bombarded with the stereotype of the perfect female image: a voluptuous body measuring 38-24-36, with large breasts, shapely hips, large buttocks and perfect skin devoid of acne, pimples, stretch marks and varicose veins. This stereotype is spoon-fed to humanity by the media—namely magazines, music lyrics, beauty contests, movies and television shows. The average woman perceives this picture and believes this is what she is supposed to be and what her husband really wants. After repeated failures to achieve this impossibility, she becomes totally frustrated and gives up because she cannot compete with nor compare to a pin-up fantasy girl. As a result, she loses more and more self-esteem and personal confidence. Once a wife's Body Shape Image (**BSI**) level drops, her Daily Sexual Appetite (**DSA**) level also decreases proportionally. This handbook is written to reverse this trend and stop the cycle of rejection.

I believe that with the help of this handbook, the Word of God and the Holy Spirit, every woman will learn to love every inch, every foot, every ounce and every pound of her body—unconditionally and uncritically.

You may be asking yourself, "Why is a man so concerned about a woman's self-image?" or, "Why is Apostle Greenup so determined to help women develop a good, positive image of their bodies? The answer is very simple. I am married to a woman. The way my wife feels about her body directly affects me and how she fulfills my sexual needs through our lovemaking.

As a pastor, for many years my first love after Jesus Christ was my church—Christ the Deliverer Assembly in Baton Rouge, Louisiana. During that period, I was not attentive to my wife or her needs. I was not sensitive to her feelings, hurts or pain. This went on for a long time.

Our first baby, Joel, died of crib death at the age of seven months. Unfortunately, I didn't spend much time with him. My wife conceived again and the time came for delivery. For the birth of our second son, Josiah, I dropped my wife off at the hospital to deliver the baby alone while I attended to church business. It wasn't until the birth of our third son, Daniel, that the Lord spoke to me and told me to attend the delivery with my wife.

All three of my boys were brought into this world by Caesarean section. When I finally witnessed what my wife experienced and endured to deliver my three sons, God opened my eyes and gave me a new and deep appreciation for her. The scars on her body from the three Caesarean sections were a sign and continual reminder of her love for me. It was as if our marriage was "born again." I began to court and romance my wife the way I used to when we first met. I openly demonstrated my love for her. I told Karen that I loved her and every part of her body.

That is when God inspired the slogans, "A Sexy Spouse Makes a Happy House" and "I've Got a Good Thing at Home; My Mind Don't Need to Roam." I began to admire and appreciate my wife's body along with her scars and stretch marks which were caused by three pregnancies and Caesarean section deliveries. As a result, her confidence in her appearance returned and an aggressiveness in sex increased. Needless to say, my wife went from mild to WILD!

As you read this handbook and practice the principles herein, you will learn to love your body as it is now. Then, after you implement the activities and exercises outlined, you will pamper your body and nourish it like never before—to achieve its best possible physical potential. So, throw out that old stereotype, take a deep breath and let's get started on a lovelier you!

NOTE: *This handbook is not a substitute for regular physical checkups and professional medical advice.*

I Love My Body!

MRS. KAREN H. GREENUP
(a.k.a. *"Nurse Good Thing"*)

CHAPTER ONE

FROM HEAD TO TOE,
LOVE MUST FLOW

*"True love for your body starts in your heart,
for real beauty begins within."*

CHAPTER ONE

FROM HEAD TO TOE, LOVE MUST FLOW

Loving yourself makes a lovelier you. When a woman learns to love and appreciate herself, her physical appearance will change and improve. How will this happen? It's very simple. When you change your perception of yourself, the words that you speak over your life will also change.

Your words are very powerful. The Bible says death and life exist in your tongue, out of the abundance of the heart the mouth speaks and out of the heart proceed the issues of life. You must begin to see yourself as lovely and beautiful. Then, speak these positive, life-changing words to yourself. True love for your body starts in your heart, for real beauty begins within. For as a woman thinks in her heart, so is she. To affect a change on the outside, you must continually speak words of life about yourself and to yourself. Love from your heart will cover a multitude of shortcomings including scars, cellulite and varicose veins.

The secular world understands the power of positive words to effect life and change circumstances. Most laugh at the plant lover who encourages others to speak to plants in loving tones using encouraging words. But, there is documented evidence of success using this technique to enhance plant growth.

Let's apply this truth to yourself as a woman. When you are complimented, you begin to glow and radiate inner beauty. But, when you're not appreciated, your countenance drops and the glow quickly fades. If you love your body, your body will love you. When you love your body, you speak truth, life, health, strength, energy, vitality, beauty and longevity into every cell, tissue and organ of your body. But, when you hate your body, you speak lies, death, sickness, weakness, fatigue, depression, ugliness and premature death into every cell, tissue and organ of your body.

Loving yourself as God commanded you to is not carnal. On the contrary, loving yourself is the gauge used to love others. In Matthew 22:39, God commands all people to *"love thy neighbor as thyself...."* If you love yourself, it's easy to love others. But, if you hate yourself, you have no love for others. How can you love another person whom God has made but hate yourself whom God has also made?

Love is the most powerful force in the earth. The presence of love inspires and encourages women to be the best they can be. However, the opposite of this is also true. The absence of love creates an atmosphere of depression and low self-esteem. To overcome this state, an individual must

L♥ve N♥tes F♥r Y♥ur B♥dy

_____

_____

_____

_____

_____

_____

_____

_____

_____

_____

_____

_____

_____

_____

_____

_____

_____

_____

_____

_____

_____

_____

_____

- ♥ love <u>what</u> God has made you—a <u>woman</u>;

- ♥ love <u>who</u> God has made you—a <u>wife</u>; and

- ♥ love <u>why</u> God has made you—a <u>winner</u>!

FIVE ALIVE!

In the English language, the word "love" is a very generic and general term. It is used to describe intense feelings for both animate and inanimate objects. The word "love" is used to describe feelings for our parents, children, spouses, cats, dogs and goldfish. This one word is used to express intense feelings for a wide range of people, objects and things.

Within the Greek language, there are five words that describe the word "love." These words are ***agape, phileo, storge, epithumia and eros***. Each of these five words describes different kinds or types of love, which makes the definition more distinct and clear. You must learn to love and appreciate your body with each of these five types of love.

You must learn not to see your body as a thing of embarrassment or shame. It is not to be abused or misused by you or anyone else. And it is not to be viewed as a weight or burden until you receive your glorified body in heaven. You are to love, care for, appreciate and preserve your earthly tabernacle right now! The Bible confirms this in 2 Corinthians 4:7 for God's treasure is in His earthen vessels. In this epistle, the Apostle Paul revealed that God has deposited His treasure or divine power within your physical body. If God esteems your body enough to place His treasure in it, who are you to despise it?

It's time to revive your body with **Five Alive!** It's time to love and appreciate your body for its natural beauty and worth. I guarantee that if you begin to love your body with the aforementioned five types of love and repeat the love affirmations listed below, you will see a dramatic transformation in your physical appearance.

AGAPE

This is God's-kind of love. God demonstrated agape by loving humanity while we were yet sinners. "Agape" is unconditional love. You must love your body regardless of its current shape. You must love all the extra pounds, sags and scars right now! And you must love it in an uncritical and non-judgmental way.

L♥ve N♥tes F♥r Y♥ur B♥dy

_____

_____

_____

_____

_____

_____

_____

_____

_____

_____

_____

_____

_____

_____

_____

_____

_____

_____

_____

_____

_____

_____

_____

_____

LOVE AFFIRMATION #1 (SAY OUT LOUD)

"I love my body with an unconditional,
uncritical and unlimited love."

PHILEO

This is the friendship kind of love. You must know your body as you know a friend. You must accept your body as a friend. You must be your body's ally and supporter. And you must like your body and be fond of it.

LOVE AFFIRMATION #2 (SAY OUT LOUD)

"I like my body. My body is my best friend.
I do not compare it to others. I will not compete with others."

STORGE

This is social love. "Storge" is the kind of love you feel for your family: your children, parents, brothers and sisters. It is the kind of love that develops and exists as the result of a close connection or relationship. This may sound strange, but you must be as close to your body and know it as well as your own children.

LOVE AFFIRMATION #3 (SAY OUT LOUD)

"I know every detail of my body and I love it.
I will nurture and cherish my body for it is part of my total being."

EPITHUMIA

This is the sensual type of love which can be described as a holy kind of lust. "Epithumia" is the strong desire and passion that's a part of your physical make-up. You must love and enjoy the sensual feelings of your body. Love the way it looks. Love the way it feels. Love the way it smells. And love the sexual desires that arise in your body in response to your husband's love, affection and touch.

LOVE AFFIRMATION #4 (SAY OUT LOUD)

"I love the way my body looks, feels and smells.
I am enthusiastic and excited about my body and who I am."

L♥ve N♥tes F♥r Y♥ur B♥dy

_____

_____

_____

_____

_____

_____

_____

_____

_____

_____

_____

_____

_____

_____

_____

_____

_____

_____

_____

_____

_____

_____

_____

_____

EROS

This is erotic, sexual love. "Eros" is manifested as the physical expression of intercourse between a husband and wife in a monogamous relationship. You must learn to love and appreciate sexual intercourse with your spouse. This intimate experience is reserved for married couples alone. Sex with your husband is not wrong, shameful or sinful. On the contrary, God created it to be beautiful and wonderful.

LOVE AFFIRMATION #5 (SAY OUT LOUD)

"I am a sexual being. I enjoy the pleasure and sexual arousal I experience from my husband's touch. I am R.A.W. (ready, always and willing; and romantic, aggressive and wild). I am not cold, frigid or inhibited in regards to sexual love."

I LOVE MY BODY, I LOVE MY BEAUTY

Unfortunately, most women have a negative body image. Because they do not measure up to the "Hollywood" and media image, most women are over-critical of their bodies. When asked, most women can rattle off a list of complaints, faults and shortcomings about their bodies. Regardless of how others may perceive her, the average woman has a negative self-image of her body. Most women feel that they are either too tall or too short, too fat or too thin, too dark or too light. They are unhappy with themselves and the way God made them. They verbally express their negative opinions so often that it effects their actions in public and private places. For example, the average wife is:

- ♥ afraid to be seen in public.
- ♥ self-conscious about the way she looks when fully dressed.
- ♥ ashamed to wear certain types of lingerie.
- ♥ embarrassed to be totally nude before her husband.
- ♥ afraid to take a shower or bathe with her husband.
- ♥ afraid to make love with the lights on.
- ♥ ashamed of trying different sexual positions.

All of these "feelings" are psychological, mental and emotional hindrances to total sexual satisfaction. Wives, let me share a secret with you. A man's greatest turn-on is a confident, self-assured woman. The most appealing thing to a hus-

L♥ve N♥tes F♥r Y♥ur B♥dy

_____

_____

_____

_____

_____

_____

_____

_____

_____

_____

_____

_____

_____

_____

_____

_____

_____

_____

_____

_____

_____

_____

band is a woman who is sure of herself and confident in her ability to attract and satisfy her mate. It's not what you have, what you don't have or even how attractive you are that counts. Rather, it's how you feel and use what you have that really matters. Nothing is more attractive to a husband than a self-confident, self-loving and selfless wife.

Most wives feel like **U.F.O.'s**—an Unattractive, Fat Object or Ugly, Fat and Old. Do you feel like either of these UFO's? Do you hate what you see when you look in the mirror? Let me show you how to properly identify a **UFO**. A woman who is a UFO has

- ♥ no love from above.
- ♥ no heart to start.
- ♥ no fire of desire.
- ♥ no passion for fashion.
- ♥ no affection for connection.
- ♥ no heat to meet.
- ♥ no urge to merge.
- ♥ no attraction for action.
- ♥ no unction to function.
- ♥ no energy for ecstasy.
- ♥ no need to breed.

Do any of these characteristics describe you? If so, read on. Wives who feel oversized also feel undersexed. This type of UFO feels frigid and rigid, old and cold, neglected and rejected, dumb and numb and/or bored and ignored. She ends up being a deadhead in bed, has no enthusiasm for orgasm and cannot relax to climax.

Women of God, let me share another secret with you. Sex begins in the mind. Remember, as a woman thinks in her heart, so is she. If a wife thinks she is unattractive, ugly and fat, she will dress accordingly. How she acts depends on her thoughts—whether they are good or bad. And every thought will eventually manifest itself as an action. If you think you're ugly, you'll act like you're ugly. If you think you're fat, you'll act as though you're fat. And if you think you're old, you'll act old. However, if you think you're beautiful, you'll act like you're beautiful. If you think you're fine and shapely, you'll act as though you're fine and shapely. And if you think you're young, you'll act young.

L♥ve N♥tes F♥r Y♥ur B♥dy

_____

_____

_____

_____

_____

_____

_____

_____

_____

_____

_____

_____

_____

_____

_____

_____

_____

_____

_____

_____

_____

_____

_____

L♥ve N♥tes F♥r Y♥ur B♥dy

Every woman should have and exercise the attitude and mind of love. 1 Corinthians 13:5 says that God's-kind of love thinks no evil. If you believe this truth, you won't think evil about yourself. For agape love only thinks beautiful thoughts. In addition, Philippians 4:8 instructs women to think on things that are true, just, pure, lovely, virtuous and of a good report. In Acts 26:2, the Apostle Paul said, *"I think myself happy...."* Paul thought for himself. He didn't allow others to think for him. Women must think like Paul did.

Even God the Father is thinking good thoughts about you. In Isaiah 55:8, God said His thoughts are not the same as your thoughts. God only thinks good thoughts about you and your body for it is His prize creation. In Jeremiah 29:11, the Bible tells us that God thinks thoughts of peace about you—not evil. Begin to think God's thoughts about yourself.

Don't be the wrong kind of **UFO**, become the right kind of **UFO**. A Unique, Feminine Organism (a beautiful human being) who Understands Female Organs (her sexual parts and functions) and experiences the Ultimate Female Orgasm (total satisfaction from clitoral and vaginal stimulation).

L♥ve N♥tes F♥r Y♥ur B♥dy

_____

_____

_____

_____

_____

_____

_____

_____

_____

_____

_____

_____

_____

_____

_____

_____

_____

_____

_____

_____

_____

_____

AGAPE LOVE AFFIRMATIONS

You must renew your mind (Romans 12:2) and think lovely things (Philippians 4:8) about your body because you will become what you think in your heart (Proverbs 23:7). Change the way you think about your body by reciting the following affirmations everyday.

"I love my body."

"I love my flesh."

"I love my skin."

"I love my hair."

"I love my face."

"I love my eyes."

"I love my nose."

"I love my ears."

"I love my lips."

"I love my cheeks."

"I love my neck."

"I love my shoulders."

"I love my arms."

"I love my elbows."

"I love my hands."

"I love my fingers."

"I love my nails."

"I love my breasts."

"I love my nipples."

"I love my stomach."

"I love my navel."

"I love my pelvis."

"I love my pubic hair."

"I love my mound."

"I love my genitals."

"I love my vagina."

"I love my labia."

"I love my clitoris."

"I love my back."

"I love my buttocks."

"I love my hips."

"I love my thighs."

"I love my legs."

"I love my knees."

"I love my calves."

"I love my ankles."

"I love my feet."

"I love my toes."

I love myself!

L♥ve N♥tes F♥r Y♥ur B♥dy

_____

_____

_____

_____

_____

_____

_____

_____

_____

_____

_____

_____

_____

_____

_____

_____

_____

_____

_____

_____

_____

_____

L♥ve N♥tes F♥r Y♥ur B♥dy

PHILEO LOVE AFFIRMATIONS

You must accept, admire, appreciate and adore your body as your best friend. Learn to like your body as your favorite intimate companion. Change the perception of your body by reciting the following affirmations everyday.

"I like my body."
"I like my flesh."
"I like my skin."
"I like my hair."
"I like my face."
"I like my eyes."
"I like my nose."
"I like my ears."
"I like my lips."
"I like my cheeks."
"I like my neck."
"I like my shoulders."
"I like my arms."
"I like my elbows."
"I like my hands."
"I like my fingers."
"I like my nails."
"I like my breasts."
"I like my nipples."
"I like my stomach."

"I like my navel."
"I like my pelvis."
"I like my pubic hair."
"I like my mound."
"I like my genitals."
"I like my vagina."
"I like my labia."
"I like my clitoris."
"I like my back."
"I like my buttocks."
"I like my hips."
"I like my thighs."
"I like my legs."
"I like my knees."
"I like my calves."
"I like my ankles."
"I like my feet."
"I like my toes."

I like myself!

L♥ve N♥tes F♥r Y♥ur B♥dy

_____

_____

_____

_____

_____

_____

_____

_____

_____

_____

_____

_____

_____

_____

_____

_____

_____

_____

_____

_____

CHAPTER TWO

GOD MADE ALL THINGS BEAUTIFUL

"The psalmist David said that we are fearfully and wonderfully made. God made every part of you beautiful."

CHAPTER TWO

GOD MADE ALL THINGS BEAUTIFUL

In Ecclesiastes 3:11, God declared that He made everything beautiful. As the Creator, God made everything visible and invisible—and made it all beautiful. The creation described in the book of Genesis outlines six days of beautiful creation.

In the beginning, God looked at the earth and it was void and without form. On the first day, God created day and night; and God called it good. On the second day, God created the sky and the ocean; and God called it good. On the third day, God created the earth, the seas and all of the trees, grass and plants; and God called it good. On the fourth day, God created the sun, moon and stars; and God called it good. On the fifth day, God created the animals and fish; and God called it good.

On the sixth day, God created man. Genesis 1:27 reveals that God made man in His image as both male and female. God looked at everything He created and said, *"very good."* Then God rested from His labor.

Everything that God created from day one to day five, He called good. But, only after He created man as male and female did He say, *"very good."* On the sixth day, God called man and woman *"very good."* Man was created in the wonderful and fearful similitude of God. This means that God made every part of you beautiful.

Eve was created from Adam's side and existed naked with her husband for a time. During that period, she had no fears, hang-ups or inhibitions. Eve was beautiful, naked and without shame before the fall. Only after their sin did Adam and Eve attempt to cover themselves and hide from God's presence. Let me reveal something to you. Every Christian woman is a daughter of Eve. Today, Eve is an example of how all women of God must view themselves and their body.

M.A.D. BODY INSTRUCTION

I believe that Christian mothers must wake up and realize the damage some of them are doing to their daughter's body image. It's time to have some **M.A.D.** instruction in Christian homes. M.A.D. is an acronym that stands for Mothers And Daughters. Mothers are chiefly responsible for teaching their daughters to love, like and appreciate their body.

I'm sure that many Christian and non-Christian ladies were shocked by the

Love Notes For Your Body

_____

_____

_____

_____

_____

_____

_____

_____

_____

_____

_____

_____

_____

_____

_____

_____

_____

_____

_____

_____

_____

_____

_____

_____

_____

Love Notes For Your Body

recent news of pop singer and dancer Paula Abdul. Paula openly discussed her self-image and problems with bulimia.

Recently on an evening talk show, Paula Abdul admitted that she battled with a very negative image of her body for the past 15 years. She admitted feeling inferior about her body size and shape since she was eight years old. It was at this impressionable age that she became interested in dance and enrolled in ballet. Paula recalled that the other girls in the class were tall and thin, whereas she was short and round. This became public knowledge when the instructor called attention to her different body shape in front of the entire class. Needless to say, Paula was completely humiliated.

Later, at the age of 16, Paula learned what she believed to be the secret of staying thin. She couldn't understand how the other dancers maintained thin bodies and still enjoyed food. They introduced Paula to a procedure called binging and purging. Simply stated, a person goes on an eating binge and then removes the food from the stomach through forced vomiting. These are the classic symptoms of the eating disorder called bulimia.

Bulimics crave and consume large amounts of food when they go on an eating binge. This binge is usually sparked by some type of emotional stress or trauma. Once the binging process is complete, the bulimic feels guilty about what she has done and is fearful of gaining weight. So, she forces herself to vomit by sticking a finger down her throat. This vicious cycle continues over and over and over again.

Paula Abdul admitted that her eating was strictly emotional. Her binges were linked to a poor image of her body. After the binge, she purged herself so she wouldn't gain any weight. Paula lived in this private torment for years until she sought professional help in July, 1994.

Since her debut to the entertainment world in 1989, Paula Abdul has been the envy of many women and the object of many men's fantasies. This sexy dancer has dated some of Hollywood's most eligible bachelors. Despite her beauty, fame and all of her dancing accomplishments, Paula Abdul saw herself as a fat girl in the mirror. In her mind, she was fat and overweight.

Of all the revelations that she shared during the interview, only one sounded an alarm in my ears. Paula stated that although her mother was a very naturally beautiful woman, she never felt thin enough. This deception transferred from mother to daughter. I believe this was the root and beginning of Paula's poor self-image.

A little girl is usually the reflection of her mother's upbringing. Ezekiel 16:44

Love Notes For Your Body

states, *"As is the mother, so is her daughter."* Whether deliberately or ignorantly, directly or indirectly, mothers help shape the attitude of their children—especially their daughters. I believe that Paula Abdul received her poor self-image from her mother's perception of herself. The negative words spoken and bad attitudes shared only solidified this lie. Her mother is not totally to blame, but her attitude cannot be ignored. Christian mothers, I implore you to take notice of Paula's plight and battle with bulimia and implement the right solution to reverse this curse with your daughters.

Older women must instruct the younger women to avoid making the same mistakes. Young girls must be taught how to love and appreciate their body. Children must be taught that their body was made by God and God makes all things beautiful. No girl should grow up hating her looks or being ashamed of her body. This is best taught at an early age by the mother in the home. Every little girl deserves to grow up feeling good about who she is, how she looks and what she was created to do.

MADE IN HIS IMAGE BUT NOT THE SAME

One major mistake that women make is to compare themselves to the world's standard of beauty and bodily perfection. The Bible tells us that they who compare and measure themselves to others are not wise. Many ladies compare themselves to a standard body shape only to realize their body does not conform to that image. Most walk away from this experience feeling like a failure and believing their body is unattractive. Nothing is further from the truth.

The truth of the matter is there are four different female body types. All women are not formed exactly the same. On the contrary, the female body type is linked to and associated with a woman's dominant hormonal gland which is inherited or determined by genetics.

The four basic female body types are: android or mesomorph; gynecoid or endomorph; lymphatic; and thyroid or ectomorph. Each of these body types has its own physical characteristics which is determined by a woman's hormonal make-up. How and where you gain weight—and how, when and where you lose weight are totally determined by your particular body type.

Read over the descriptions below and identify your unique body type.

1. Android or Mesomorph ♥ The android or mesomorph body type is the more muscular than the common female body. This type of woman has a thick skeletal frame, a large neck, shoulders, chest area and waist. The pelvis of an android woman is rather narrow. Consequently, this body type has a box-torso-shape with very few feminine curves. When an

Love Notes For Your Body

_____

_____

_____

_____

_____

_____

_____

_____

_____

_____

_____

_____

_____

_____

_____

_____

_____

_____

_____

_____

_____

_____

android type woman gains weight, it is most apparent in her upper body especially during middle age. This body type also gains weight in the abdomen area, giving a pot-belly appearance. Android types have large bones in their hands, feet and legs. They usually have more muscle mass and less fat than other body types. Because android women have higher levels of male hormones, they have excessive body and facial hair.

2. Gynecoid or Endomorph ♥ This female body type is considered to be the most voluptuous body shape. Gynecoid women have a pear-shaped body with average or small shoulders that taper to a small waist, rounded hips, thighs and buttocks. The inside thighs of a gynecoid woman generally touch and rub against each other and the bones of her pelvic area are wide for childbirth. The dominant hormone in the gynecoid woman is estrogen. The prevalence of estrogen causes the gynecoid woman to gain weight in her hips, thighs, buttocks and breasts. This results in uneven fatty tissue and excessive cellulite. Generally, gynecoid women are very fertile and become pregnant very easily.

3. Lymphatic ♥ The lymphatic type woman has a puffy-looking body because it retains water very easily. Her face is generally round and her neck is rather short. The water retention and fatty tissues under the skin cause her arms and legs to have a same-size or straight-up-and-down appearance. The shoulders and breasts of a lymphatic woman are average size and the abdomen usually protrudes. When a lymphatic woman gains weight, it is evenly distributed all over her body including her arms, legs, ankles, face and neck. Normally, this type of woman has been overweight since childhood and suffers from a very low or sluggish metabolism. Because of this, a lymphatic woman gains weight more easily than any other body type.

4. Thyroid or Ectomorph ♥ The thyroid body type is characterized by a slender body, with long arms and legs. This type of woman appears boyish in shape. She may be tall or appear tall even if her height is average. The fingers and toes of the thyroid type are also long and slender. This type of woman is often considered "bony" from childhood. She usually excels athletically as a sprinter, basketball player or dancer. If a thyroid type gains weight, it will be noticed first around the abdomen and upper thighs. Of all the body types, the thyroid woman is the most slender with very little body fat. She is also characterized by a high or fast metabolic rate.

As you can see from the four body types described above, it is physically impossible for women to strive for one "ideal" body shape. For too many years,

Love Notes For Your Body

_____

_____

_____

_____

_____

_____

_____

_____

_____

_____

_____

_____

_____

_____

_____

_____

_____

_____

_____

_____

_____

_____

_____

_____

_____

_____

_____

Love Notes For Your Body

women have judged their own bodies by the standards of the media or Hollywood. Hollywood is in no position to reject or condemn the physical structure that God created!

It is completely ridiculous for a woman with a lymphatic body type to feel inferior to a woman with a thyroid body type; or an android type woman to feel inferior to a gynecoid body type. Instead of judging and comparing yourself, learn your body type, understand its characteristics and love it for what it is. God's masterpiece!

It is perfectly acceptable to want to lose weight or tone up, but trying to adhere to or achieve a body standard that is not your type is absurd. Know this. You cannot change your God-given body type. If your body type is android, then love it. If you need to lose weight or get in shape up, work to become the best-looking android body type you can be. Accept and love yourself for the way you are. Don't feel unattractive because you don't have the long legs and slender body of a thyroid body type. You are no less of a woman!

This type of wrong thinking was the very thing that caused Paula Abdul to experience years of anxiety and frustration as she struggled with her eating disorder. Judging by her physical appearance, Paula seems to have a gynecoid body type. However, because her shape was different from the other dancers (probably thyroid body types) she felt unattractive and unaccepted by the group which led to her problems with bulimia. Do what Susan Ponders says—"STOP THE INSANITY!" Stop thinking bad thoughts. And stop torturing yourself. You can be beautiful regardless of your body type and shape. Just be the best you can be, feel good about yourself and love your body!

L♥ve N♥tes F♥r Y♥ur B♥dy

BEAUTIFUL BODY AFFIRMATIONS

Despite what you think and how you feel about your body, you must see yourself as God does. Change the way you view every part of your body by repeating the following affirmations. Beauty comes by hearing yourself speak these truths.

"I love the beauty of my body."

"I love the beauty of my flesh."

"I love the beauty of my skin."

"I love the beauty of my hair."

"I love the beauty of my face."

"I love the beauty of my eyes."

"I love the beauty of my nose."

"I love the beauty of my ears."

"I love the beauty of my lips."

"I love the beauty of my cheeks."

"I love the beauty of my neck."

"I love the beauty of my shoulders."

"I love the beauty of my arms."

"I love the beauty of my elbows."

"I love the beauty of my hands."

"I love the beauty of my fingers."

"I love the beauty of my nails."

"I love the beauty of my breasts."

L♥ve N♥tes F♥r Y♥ur B♥dy

_____

_____

_____

_____

_____

_____

_____

_____

_____

_____

_____

_____

_____

_____

_____

_____

_____

_____

_____

_____

_____

_____

_____

"I love the beauty of my nipples."

"I love the beauty of my stomach."

"I love the beauty of my navel."

"I love the beauty of my pelvis."

"I love the beauty of my pubic hair."

"I love the beauty of my mound."

"I love the beauty of my genitals."

"I love the beauty of my vagina."

"I love the beauty of my labia."

"I love the beauty of my clitoris."

"I love the beauty of my back."

"I love the beauty of my buttocks."

"I love the beauty of my hips."

"I love the beauty of my thighs."

"I love the beauty of my legs."

"I love the beauty of my knees."

"I love the beauty of my calves."

"I love the beauty of my ankles."

"I love the beauty of my feet."

"I love the beauty of my toes."

Now hug yourself!

L♥ve N♥tes F♥r Y♥ur B♥dy

_____

_____

_____

_____

_____

_____

_____

_____

_____

_____

_____

_____

_____

_____

_____

_____

_____

_____

_____

_____

_____

_____

WHAT'S YOUR B.S.I. (Body Shape Image)?

Read the Song of Solomon. Many theologians have correctly interpreted this erotic book to be a symbolic relationship between Christ and His Church. But, according to the book of Ephesians, husbands and wives also represent Christ and the Church. The Song of Solomon is a poem or psalm that extols the beauty of human, marital relationships.

I encourage you to read this *"song of songs"* in the King James and Living versions of the Bible. In frank and open terms, the Song of Solomon should cause you to praise God for making your body—which is beautiful regardless of its type, shape, size and color. Truly, man and woman are fearfully and wonderfully made.

In this book, Abishag (Solomon's wife) was not ashamed to be naked or noisy with her husband. She was a vision of pleasure and a voice of praise to him. Abishag gave Solomon <u>eyerotic</u> appreciation, <u>earotic</u> affirmation, visual admiration and verbal adoration. Abishag did this because she had a very high **B.S.I.** level. You might ask yourself, "What's a B.S.I. level?" B.S.I. is an acronym which stands for your **BODY SHAPE-IMAGE,** your **BODY SIZE-IMAGE,** your **BODY SELF-IMAGE** and your **BODY SEX-IMAGE.** You can change your current BSI level by speaking the following affirmations everyday.

- ♥ I will learn my body—its parts, organs, purposes, uses and functions.
- ♥ I will love my body—its size, shape, features and figure.
- ♥ I will love my body—its passion, pleasure, feelings and desires.
- ♥ I will look at my body—without fear, shame, disgust or embarrassment.
- ♥ I will laugh at my body—its flaws, imperfections, defects and scars.
- ♥ I will loose my body—from all negative thoughts, past hang-ups, old habits and emotional scars.

The Song of Solomon is a beautiful portrayal of man who is made in God's image and woman as his help meet. The sexual relationship described in this book is the ultimate expression of God's love between a husband and wife and must be expressed openly and freely.

The Song of Solomon is:

- ♥ a love song to make your marriage strong;
- ♥ a love letter to make your sex life better;
- ♥ a love dance of sweet romance; and
- ♥ a love story for God's glory.

L♥ve N♥tes F♥r Y♥ur B♥dy

_____

_____

_____

_____

_____

_____

_____

_____

_____

_____

_____

_____

_____

_____

_____

_____

_____

_____

_____

_____

_____

_____

_____

_____

The Song of Solomon is a book of:

- ♥ Meditation—it puts your mind in the mood—Admiration;
- ♥ Motivation—it puts your muscles in motion—Activation; and
- ♥ Medication—it works a miracle in your marriage—Appreciation.

UGLINESS IS NOT HOLINESS

Unfortunately, a belief exists in the Church that a woman has to be drab, plain, common and ugly to be holy. Wrong! You don't have to be ugly to be holy. Ugliness is not linked to godliness.

I believe this idea exists because the Church is afraid to acknowledge, accept and embrace the ideas and concepts of the world. The Church knows that the world is engrossed with looks and physical beauty—adorning themselves with clothes, jewels, make-up and other accessories. Because this is how the world acts, the Church believes that it must act in the opposite manner. For the world is concerned with earthly things and the Church with heavenly things; the world is full of hate and violence and the Church is supposed to be filled with love and peace.

It seems logical that if the world concentrates on beauty, bodily adornments and looking good, the Church must take the opposite stance. Consequently, many Christian women (especially those in Pentecostal churches) believe they shouldn't adorn themselves physically. It is even preached that women should not wear make-up or jewelry but drab clothing. Surely, this concept did not come from God or the Bible.

In Ezekiel 16:10-14, God recounts how He singlehandedly made Israel great. I realize God is speaking symbolically in this passage, but He did not use evil symbols to illustrate His love for Israel. In these verses, God reminded Israel how He clothed her with fine linen and silk garments, decked her with bracelets and necklaces and decorated her with jewels and a beautiful crown. God beautified Israel with the precious metals of gold and silver. However, Israel let her favor and beauty go to her head. She became lifted up with pride and went whoring after other gods. The sin of Israel was pride—not looking beautiful.

Please realize that all things must be done in moderation. For a false balance is an abomination to the Lord. God wants us to be balanced in all aspects of our lives.

God has a special type of beauty reserved for Christian women. He wants us to be adorned with the **beauty of holiness.** This beauty radiates from the inside out. It originates from the Holy Spirit and is manifest in your countenance. God

L♥ve N♥tes F♥r Y♥ur B♥dy

_____

_____

_____

_____

_____

_____

_____

_____

_____

_____

_____

_____

_____

_____

_____

_____

_____

_____

_____

_____

_____

_____

_____

wants us to be beautiful on the inside (our heart, our mind and our attitude) and beautiful on the outside (dressed in flattering clothing, appropriate jewelry and becoming hair styles). God wants us to be beauties of the spirit and beauties of the skin.

How could anyone think or believe that God does not want women to look beautiful? Let's briefly analyze the women in the Bible:

Eve ♥	*was the most beautiful woman who ever lived because she was hand-made by God as a glorified human being (Genesis 2:21-25).*
Sarah ♥	*was so beautiful that two different kings tried to steal her from her husband Abraham (Genesis 12:11-16, 20:1-7).*
Rachel ♥	*was so beautiful that Isaac lied and said she was his sister so the city dwellers wouldn't kill him and abduct his wife (Genesis 26:6-7).*
Abigail ♥	*the wife of Nabal the drunkard, was not only beautiful but also wise to marry David after her first husband's death (1 Samuel 25:3).*
Bathsheba ♥	*the wife of Urriah the Hittite was very beautiful to look upon as King David discovered (2 Samuel 11:2).*
Tamar ♥	*the beautiful daughter of David was raped by her own brother Amnon (2 Samuel 13:1).*
Vashti ♥	*was so beautiful her husband the king wanted to publicly display her before the men and governors of the royal court (Esther 1:11).*
Esther ♥	*was so beautiful that she won a beauty contest, became the queen and interceded for the nation of Israel (Esther 2:7-17).*
Abishag ♥	*was so beautiful that she captured the heart of King Solomon (Song of Solomon 1:6, 1:15-16, 2:10, 4:1-10, 6:4).*

All of the biblical heroines mentioned above were beautiful. In the case of Esther, she spent one year purifying and beautifying herself before she was presented to the king. There is nothing wrong with or evil about enhancing your looks by using make-up.

Many opponents of cosmetics defend their spiritual position with the biblical account of Jezebel. 2 Kings 9:30 recounts how Jezebel painted her face in preparation for the arrival of King Jehu. The Bible identifies Jezebel as an evil woman and Jesus called her a seducing false prophetess. Despite these truths, it was not the fact that Jezebel painted her face or wore make-up that made her

L♥ve N♥tes F♥r Y♥ur B♥dy

_____

_____

_____

_____

_____

_____

_____

_____

_____

_____

_____

_____

_____

_____

_____

_____

_____

_____

_____

_____

_____

_____

evil. It was because of her rebellious heart and that she usurped God's authority and divine government.

Let me ask you something. Is it a sin to paint your house if it looks drab and listless? The answer is no. Is it a sin to wax your car if it has lost its luster? No. Why then does religion considered it a sin to use make-up to improve your looks? We beautify our homes and spruce up our cars when they need it. Why not apply make-up to enhance your looks? Sometimes, a woman needs *make-up* to *wake-up* her natural beauty.

L♥ve N♥tes F♥r Y♥ur B♥dy

_____

_____

_____

_____

_____

_____

_____

_____

_____

_____

_____

_____

_____

_____

_____

_____

_____

_____

_____

_____

_____

_____

_____

BEAUTY AFFIRMATIONS

It's time to change your attitude and raise your **BSI** level. You must learn to love your body for it's the only one you will have this side of heaven. Begin by repeating and believing these affirmations.

My body is beautiful.

My flesh is beautiful.

My skin is beautiful.

My hair is beautiful.

My face is beautiful.

My eyes are beautiful.

My nose is beautiful.

My ears are beautiful.

My lips are beautiful.

My cheeks are beautiful.

My neck is beautiful.

My shoulders are beautiful.

My arms are beautiful.

My elbows are beautiful.

My hands are beautiful.

My fingers are beautiful.

My nails are beautiful.

My breasts are beautiful.

My nipples are beautiful.

My stomach is beautiful.

My navel is beautiful.

My pelvis is beautiful.

My pubic hair is beautiful.

My mound is beautiful.

My genitals are beautiful.

My vagina is beautiful.

My labia are beautiful.

My clitoris is beautiful.

My back is beautiful.

My buttocks are beautiful.

My hips are beautiful.

My thighs are beautiful.

My legs are beautiful.

My knees are beautiful.

My calves are beautiful.

My ankles are beautiful.

My feet are beautiful.

My toes are beautiful.

I am beautiful!

L♥ve N♥tes F♥r Y♥ur B♥dy

_____

_____

_____

_____

_____

_____

_____

_____

_____

_____

_____

_____

_____

_____

_____

_____

_____

_____

_____

_____

I am beautiful!

I am gorgeous!

I am lovely!

I am pretty!

I am fine!

(Repeat these affirmations only if they apply)

I may be big, but I'm beautiful!

I may be large, but I'm lovely!

I may be plump, but I'm pretty!

I may be chubby, but I'm cute!

I may be fat, but I'm fine!

I may be huge, but I'm horny!

L♥ve N♥tes F♥r Y♥ur B♥dy

CHAPTER THREE

A 'B.A.' DEGREE
CONCERNING MY ANATOMY

*"You cannot fully love and appreciate
anything without knowledge of that object."*

CHAPTER THREE

A 'B.A.' DEGREE
CONCERNING MY ANATOMY

Most women are totally uninformed when it comes to knowing and understanding their body. Even basic knowledge of the body and its functions seem to have eluded most women, especially wives. Women seem content to entrust their lives to doctors and their bodies to gynecologists. This explains why hysterectomies are at an all- time-high and the most common, non-emergency surgery performed today. Because a woman is uninformed or ill-informed, she accepts the diagnosis of her doctor as law without researching the problem or seeking a second opinion. This type of male-practice often leads to malpractice.

A vital part of your body affirmation program is knowing your body and how it works. You cannot fully love and appreciate anything without knowledge of that object. Your 'B.A.' degree in anatomy will include body aptitude, body attention, body acceptance, body activation and body appreciation.

Our bodies carry out a daily routine of functions that keep us alive and active. These functions are classified into the nine body systems described below. I will give a brief definition of each of these systems.

THE SKELETAL SYSTEM

The skeletal system gives the body its shape. It protects delicate organs, forms blood, stores minerals and provides the structure to which muscles are attached. The skeletal system includes the skull, ribs, spinal column, shoulder girdle, sternum, pelvic girdle and the upper and lower extremities (arms and legs).

THE MUSCULAR SYSTEM

The muscular system produces body heat, determines your posture and provides body movement. Your muscles make up a large part of your body. The muscular system includes your skeletal muscles (voluntary muscles that control body movement), involuntary muscles (muscles controlled by your automatic nervous system which are located in the walls of your internal organs) and the cardiac muscle which is found in your heart and causes it to beat and pump blood every second of your life.

THE CIRCULATORY SYSTEM

The circulatory system carries oxygen and nourishment to the cells in your

L♥ve N♥tes F♥r Y♥ur B♥dy

_____

_____

_____

_____

_____

_____

_____

_____

_____

_____

_____

_____

_____

_____

_____

_____

_____

_____

_____

_____

_____

_____

_____

_____

_____

body and waste material away from your cells. This system includes your arteries, veins and capillaries through which blood flows to your heart, spleen, lymph nodes and lymphatic vessels.

As the heart pumps, blood is circulated throughout your body. The spleen stores red blood cells and filters the blood that passes through it. Lymph nodes are tiny structures that produce white blood cells and antibodies which defend the body against harmful bacteria. Lymph vessels parallel the veins in your body and are connected to large lymph vessels which carry lymph (a fluid that washes the space between cells).

THE RESPIRATORY SYSTEM

The respiratory system acquires oxygen for your body and rids it of carbon dioxide. The respiratory system includes the lungs, nose, bronchi, trachea, pharynx and larynx.

The lungs inhale air from the external surroundings, extract the essential oxygen for the body and exhale the remaining, unused air as carbon dioxide. The nose receives air through two nostrils and simultaneously filters dust and dirt particles. The bronchi are two divisions of the windpipe that lead to the right and left lungs. The trachea is the windpipe that allows the passage of oxygen to the lungs. It also traps inhaled dust particles and dislodges them by sneezing, coughing or vomiting. The larynx is the vocal box which produces the human voice. It regulates the pitch and volume of voice through tension on the vocal cords. The pharynx is commonly called the throat. It serves as the passageway for food and air.

THE DIGESTIVE SYSTEM

The digestive system prepares food to be absorbed and used by the cells in your body. The digestive system includes the mouth, pharynx (throat), esophagus, stomach, intestines, liver, gallbladder and pancreas.

The mouth receives food which is broken down into smaller pieces through chewing and passed to the digestive tract. The pharynx or throat muscles constrict and force the food into the esophagus. The esophagus is a muscular tube that extends from the throat to the stomach where food passes. The stomach is an elastic bag where digestion and storage of food takes place. The intestines receive the undigested food from the stomach and break it down so that it can be absorbed into the bloodstream. The intestines also eliminate the part of food known as waste which cannot be used by the body. The liver and gallbladder aid in the breaking down of fats in the digestive process. The liver produces bile which breaks down fats and passes them to the gallbladder where they are

L♥ve N♥tes F♥r Y♥ur B♥dy

_____

_____

_____

_____

_____

_____

_____

_____

_____

_____

_____

_____

_____

_____

_____

_____

_____

_____

_____

_____

_____

_____

_____

_____

stored. The pancreas produces juices that digest protein, starch and fats in the small intestines.

THE ENDOCRINE SYSTEM

The endocrine system manufactures the hormones that regulate organ activities. The endocrine system includes the thyroid, parathyroid, pituitary and adrenal glands, pancreas, ovaries in women and gonads and testes in men.

The thyroid gland is located in the anterior part of the neck and regulates body metabolism (digestion of food and release of energy). The parathyroids are four tiny glands attached to the thyroid that maintain the calcium phosphorus balance in the body. The pituitary gland is located at the base of the brain. It is called the "master gland" because it helps maintain the proper function of the entire body. The pituitary gland stimulates the growth and secretion of the thyroid glands (control body metabolism), stimulates the growth of the ovarian follicles (eggs) in the female and the production of sperm in the male, stimulates ovulation (the release of an egg) from the ovaries every month, stimulates the secretion of milk and accelerates body growth—particularly long bones. The adrenal glands are located at the top of each kidney. They produce sex hormones and help the body to resist and reduce everyday stress. The adrenal glands also produce adrenaline which is a powerful cardiac stimulant. The pancreas helps digest protein, starch and fats in the small intestines. The gonads include the ovaries in women and the testes in men. The ovaries produce progesterone which is necessary for ovulation and the development of female characteristics. The testes produce testosterone which develops male characteristics. The gonads are responsible for fertility and reproduction in females and males.

THE NERVOUS SYSTEM

The nervous system communicates, coordinates and controls all of the activities of the body. The nervous system includes the brain, spinal cord, nerves and ganglia.

The brain is the master computer of the human body. It is the organ of thought which coordinates the nervous system, receives stimuli from your body organs, interprets that stimuli and forms the motor response. The spinal cord is soft and lies within the spinal column. It acts as a reflex center and pathway to and from the brain. The nerves carry impulses from the organs to the brain or spinal cord (sensory nerves), or from the brain or spinal cord to muscles or glands (motor nerves). Ganglia are masses of nerve cell bodies outside of the brain and spinal cord which carry impulses to smooth muscles, secretory glands and the heart muscle.

L♥ve N♥tes F♥r Y♥ur B♥dy

_____
_____
_____
_____
_____
_____
_____
_____
_____
_____
_____
_____

_____
_____
_____
_____
_____
_____
_____
_____
_____

THE EXCRETORY SYSTEM

The excretory system removes waste products from the body that are the results of digestion, absorption and the release of energy. The excretory system includes the skin, lungs, kidneys, ureters, bladder, urethra, bowel, rectum and anus.

The skin is the external protective covering of the body. It helps regulate body temperature through the evaporation of perspiration. The lungs rid the body of carbon dioxide and water vapor through exhalation. The kidneys secrete, collect and discharge urine which is carried to the bladder through the ureters. The ureters are small tubes that connect the kidneys to the bladder and transport urine. The bladder stores urine until one pint is accumulated. Then, through muscle contractions, the urine is forced from the bladder to the urethra which is a narrow canal that extends to the outside opening of the body. The rectum is the lowest part of the large intestine and is connected to the anus. The anus is the passageway that runs from the rectum to the outside opening of the body. Solid waste is passed from the body through the rectum.

THE REPRODUCTION SYSTEM

The reproduction system reproduces human life. Within women, the female reproductive organs include the ovaries, Fallopian tubes, uterus, vagina, labia majora (large vaginal lips), labia minora (small vaginal lips), vulva, Skene glands, Bartholin glands and breasts.

The ovaries are two almond-shaped organs that produce the ova (egg) and the female sex hormones estrogen and progesterone. The Fallopian tubes are attached to the uterus and carry the eggs from the ovaries to the uterus. The uterus is a pear-shaped organ that receives the fertilized egg and houses the growing embryo until birth. If fertilization does not occur, the endometrium (uterine lining) is sloughed off and passed from the body through menstruation. The vagina is a three to five inch muscular organ that receives sperm during sexual intercourse and stretches for the passage of a baby during childbirth. The vulva consists of the external reproductive organs including the vagina, the outer lips (labia majora), the inner lips (labia minora), the Skene glands (two small openings that secrete fluid and lubricate the urinary opening) and the clitoris (the woman's primary sexual organ for climax). The Bartholin glands are situated at the outer opening of the vulva and produce a thin mucus that lubricates the vagina. The breasts are two mounds of fatty tissue that produce milk after childbirth.

L♥ve N♥tes F♥r Y♥ur B♥dy

_____

_____

_____

_____

_____

_____

_____

_____

_____

_____

_____

_____

_____

_____

_____

_____

_____

_____

_____

_____

_____

_____

THE NINE BODY SYSTEMS AT A GLANCE

SYSTEM	FUNCTION	ORGANS
SKELETAL	Gives shape to body; helps protect organs; provides places for muscles to attach; helps form blood; stores minerals.	206 Bones: Skull, Ribs, Spinal Column, Shoulder Girdle, Sternum, Pelvic Girdle, Upper and Lower Extremities (Arms and Legs)
MUSCULAR	Protects and supports internal organs; determines posture; produces body heat; aides in body movement.	Voluntary Muscles, Involuntary Muscles, Cardiac Muscles
CIRCULATORY	Carries blood, oxygen and nourishment to cells of the body; carries waste from cells.	Heart, Arteries, Veins, Capillaries, Spleen, Lymph Nodes, Lymphatic Vessels
RESPIRATORY	Brings oxygen into the body; removes carbon dioxide through breathing.	Lungs, Nose, Bronchi, Trachea, Pharynx, Larynx
DIGESTIVE	Prepares food for use by cells; absorbs food into the body; eliminates material that is not absorbed.	Mouth, Pharynx, Esophagus, Stomach, Intestines, Liver, Gallbladder, Pancreas
ENDOCRINE	Manufactures hormones to regulate functions of organs.	Glands (Ductless): Thyroid, Parathyroid, Pituitary, Adrenal, Pancreas, Ovaries, Testes, Gonads
NERVOUS	Communicates, coordinates and controls body activities.	Brain, Spinal Cord, Nerves, Ganglia
EXCRETORY	Removes waste products that are the results of digestion, absorption and the release of energy.	Skin, Lungs, Kidneys, Ureters, Bladder, Urethra, Bowel, Rectum, Anus
REPRODUCTIVE	Reproduces human beings.	Female: Ovaries, Fallopian Tubes, Uterus, Vagina, Labia Majora (Large Vaginal Lips), Labia Minora (Small Vaginal Lips), Vulva, Skene Glands, Bartholin Glands, Breasts Male: Penis, Scrotum, Testes, Urethra, Vas Deferens, Prostate Gland, Seminal Vesicles, Ejaculatory Duct, Epididymis, Cowpers Gland

FIGURE 2.1

L♥ve N♥tes F♥r Y♥ur B♥dy

_____

_____

_____

_____

_____

_____

_____

_____

_____

_____

_____

_____

_____

_____

_____

_____

_____

_____

_____

_____

_____

_____

_____

_____

COMMON FEMALE HEALTH PROBLEMS

Some health problems exist that are common to all women. This section will address and define these problems. The lack of this basic information causes much fear and anxiety in women. Truly, the bondage of all fear is ignorance. But, the arm of knowledge is your best weapon of defense. Unfortunately, many women perish because of the lack of knowledge.

Indeed, the human female body is unique, complex and beautiful. Understanding your body and how it functions is essential to become a Unique Female Organism (UFO) and to raise your Body Self-Image (BSI) which are pre-requisites to earn your Body Appreciation (B.A.) degree.

Let me make something very plain. I am **NOT** a medical doctor. For this reason, in addition to Woman Love Your Body, I advise you to pursue other avenues of research and study concerning female reproductive health such as books, articles, films and pamphlets.

YEAST INFECTION

Although yeast infections are not serious, they can be very uncomfortable. A yeast infection is caused by a fungus called Candida Aibicans. This fungus exists in normal amounts within a woman's vagina. When the fungus overflows to abnormal levels, it causes the onset of the yeast infection. This is caused by a variety of things that disrupt the normal pH balance in the vaginal area. Some of these include douching, excessive use of feminine hygiene sprays immediately after menstruation, prolonged use of antibiotics or eating a lot of carbohydrates. The basic symptom of a yeast infection is a vaginal discharge that has a cheese-like appearance and a disagreeable odor. This is normally accompanied by an itchy rash on the vulva area. Yeast infections can be effectively treated with anti-fungal creams like Monistat, which are inserted directly into the vagina.

Despite this health problem, there are things you can do to reduce and eliminate the reoccurrence of yeast infections.

1. Wear cotton panties or cotton crouch underwear and try to limit how often you wear pantyhose. Nylon panties and pantyhose trap moisture in the vulva area and don't allow air to circulate. This provides a perfect breeding ground for the yeast fungus.

2. Limit your amount of douching, the use of bath oils and feminine hygiene sprays. These products upset the normal pH balance in the vaginal area.

3. Avoid wearing tight slacks, jeans and girdles.

4. Keep the vulva area clean and dry.

Love Notes For Your Body

ENDOMETRIOSIS

Endometriosis is known as the "career woman's disease." The endometrium is the protein-rich lining of the uterus which swells each month in preparation for pregnancy. If fertilization does not occur, the lining and the unfertilized egg are passed out through the vagina. This is called menstruation or the menstrual flow.

Pregnancy causes an interruption of this monthly cycle and stops the release of the hormones that initiate this process. In some women, when there is no pregnancy or hormonal interruption, the endometrium tissue starts to build up over time and attaches itself to other areas outside of the uterus. Heredity may also be a factor in the occurrence of this problem. Common symptoms of endometriosis include excessive menstrual cramping, heavy menstrual bleeding and irregular bleeding patterns. In addition, endometriosis can scar the Fallopian tubes or ovaries which causes infertility in women. Medical treatment for endometriosis includes pregnancy, hormone suppression treatment and/or surgery (laparoscopy).

FIBROID TUMORS

Fibroid tumors are noncancerous tumors that are found within the uterus. The development of fibroid tumors is related to the production of the hormone estrogen. Consequently, the possibility and growth rate of fibroid tumors increases in pregnant women and those who use birth control pills. When a fibroid tumor exists and grows in the uterus, the uterus will try to expel it through multiple contractions during the menstrual cycle. This causes severe menstrual cramps and bleeding, back pain, pain in the kidney area, infertility or miscarriage. Medical treatment for large uterine fibroid tumors is surgical removal or a hysterectomy.

PREMENSTRUAL SYNDROME (PMS)

PMS refers to a physical and emotional condition that recurs each month during the menstrual cycle. The onset of PMS symptoms usually begins seven to ten days prior to the start of the menstrual flow. These symptoms include irritability, tension, depression, mood swings, forgetfulness, muscle pain, cramps, headaches, food craving, bowel problems, weight gain, crying spells, fatigue, insomnia, swelling and tenderness of the breasts, acne, constipation and fluctuations in the appetite.

No one knows for sure what causes PMS. In the natural realm, it has been linked to the overproduction of estrogen and a temporary disturbance of the estrogen/progesterone balance. In the spiritual realm, PMS is linked to the curse

L♥ve N♥tes F♥r Y♥ur B♥dy

_____

_____

_____

_____

_____

_____

_____

_____

_____

_____

_____

_____

_____

_____

_____

_____

_____

_____

_____

_____

_____

_____

_____

that Eve received in Eden as a result of her sin. Suggested treatment for PMS includes changing your diet and taking vitamins—especially Vitamin E and B-6. The dietary changes include a daily intake of fish or poultry, whole grains, legumes, two servings of dairy products per day, polyunsaturated oils, an increase in green leafy vegetables, seeds and nuts. Women should limit their intake of sugar, candy, cake and pastries during this time. Other food products such as ice cream, chocolate and caffeine should also be eliminated from your diet.

PROLAPSED BLADDER, UTERUS OR RECTUM

Prolapse of a woman's bladder, uterus or rectum may be linked to a common cause-weakness in the tissue or muscles that support the pelvic area muscle group. This weakening can be caused by pregnancy, prolonged childbirth, aging or inherent weakness. In any case, the muscle fibers initially bulge into and eventually break through the vaginal wall.

The symptoms of prolapse include pain or discomfort when bearing down and the awareness of a bulge in the vaginal area. Long periods of standing can aggravate the symptoms and problem. Also, difficulty may occur when emptying the bladder, controlling urine and discharging the bowels. Surgery may be avoided by treating a prolapse with a series of exercises known as The Kegel Exercise.

In the 1950's, Dr. Arnold Kegel developed these exercises to strengthen the Pubococcygeus muscle. Doing Kegel Exercises has numerous advantages. In addition to treating and preventing organ prolapse, the exercises have been reported to improve sexual function, relieve hemorrhoids and correct stress incontinence.

To identify your Pubococcygeus (PC) muscle, the next time you urinate, sit on the toilet and try to stop the flow of urine. Another way to identify the PC muscle is to insert one of your fingers into your vagina about one-half inch to feel the muscle contract. After learning how to contract your PC muscle, do five to ten contractions each time you urinate. Over a four to six week period, you can strengthen this muscle and eliminate prolapse by increasing your contractions to 300 per day.

UTERINE CANCER

Most cancers of the uterus occur on or within the endometrium which is the lining of the uterus. Though the cause of uterine cancer is not known, there is evidence that it is linked to estrogen. The hormone progesterone causes the

L♥ve N♥tes F♥r Y♥ur B♥dy

_____

_____

_____

_____

_____

_____

_____

_____

_____

_____

_____

_____

_____

_____

_____

_____

_____

_____

_____

_____

_____

_____

_____

_____

interruption of this stimulation each month after ovulation. Use of certain birth control pills stops this process. Studies show that certain women are more likely to develop uterine cancer than others.

Known risk factors of uterine cancer include obesity, childlessness, late menopause (after age 50), diabetes, hypertension, ovarian disorders, other types of cancer, exposure to radiation, use of an estrogen replacement therapy, menstrual irregularities and inherited characteristics. In addition, women who do not ovulate frequently or those who do not get relief from constant estrogen stimulation are more likely to develop the disease. The most common symptom of uterine cancer is excessive vaginal bleeding and discharge. Medical treatment of uterine cancer involves surgery and/or radiation therapy.

BREAST CANCER

Breast cancer is the leading cause of death among women over 40 years of age. Because of this startling fact, it is important for every woman to know the warning signs of breast cancer. Some of these are a lump in the breast, underarm or area above the collarbone, a persistent skin rash, flaking or eruption near the nipple, dimpling, a pulling of the breast in one or more areas and nipple discharge which is a sudden change in the position of the nipple such as inversion.

The risk factors of this disease are a close-family history of breast cancer, previous breast or uterine cancer, radiation treatment, DES treatment during pregnancy, the beginning of a woman's menstrual period before 12 years of age and/or continuing after 55 years of age, obesity, the first pregnancy after age 30 and no previous pregnancies.

NOTE: *SURGERY SHOULD BE THE LAST RESORT FOR THE FEMALE PROBLEMS DISCUSSED IN THIS CHAPTER. OTHER HOLISTIC AND NATURAL ALTERNATIVES EXIST AND ARE REGULARLY PRACTICED BY MANY PHYSICIANS. CONSULT YOUR DOCTOR FOR MORE INFORMATION ON THESE PROVISIONAL MEDICAL APPROACHES.*

Love Notes For Your Body

_____

_____

_____

_____

_____

_____

_____

_____

_____

_____

_____

_____

_____

_____

_____

_____

_____

_____

_____

_____

_____

_____

_____

CHAPTER FOUR

FEMINIQUE:
A UNIQUE PHYSIQUE

"God created man. Then from the man's rib, He skillfully constructed woman."

CHAPTER FOUR

FEMINIQUE: A UNIQUE PHYSIQUE

The book of Genesis recounts the greatest miracle the world has ever seen—the creation of man and woman. In the beginning, God used five days to create the world including all plant and animal life. On the sixth day, God the Father, God the Son and God the Holy Spirit decided to make man in Their image. God formed man out of the dust of the ground and breathed into his nostrils the breath of life. Thus, man became a living soul. However, when God spoke of making man in Genesis 1:26, the Bible reveals, *"MALE AND FEMALE CREATED HE THEM."* God, as a Triune Being, is complete in Himself as Father, Son and Holy Ghost. God made man in His image, just like Him. God created man as a male and female in one body. This means that God and Adam had male and female characteristics.

Later, God saw that this arrangement was not good for man. Therefore, He caused a deep sleep to fall upon man. During this unconscious state, God performed the world's first surgery. He opened Adam up, removed a rib from his side, closed the man's chest and fashioned a woman. The Hebrew word used to describe the creation of man is *"baraa,"* which means to make something out of nothing. God literally created man from nothing that previously existed. On the contrary, God made the woman. The Hebrew word for *"made"* is *"banah,"* which means to build or construct from existing material. God created man. Then from the man's rib, He skillfully constructed woman.

God created woman...wo-man...or a man with a womb. He created female...female...or a male with the ability to carry a fetus. God created woman's body to conceive, bear, nurture and bring forth life.

The feminine physique is indeed unique. A comparison of the male and female sexual reproduction organs confirms their difference. The male reproductive organs serve many of the same roles as the female reproductive organs. Take the male penis for example. The penis serves as the main seat for male sexual pleasure. It is the pathway of reproduction for sperm and the passage for the elimination of urine from the body. The woman's body is also highly specialized. Take the female clitoris for example. The clitoris serves as the main seat for female sexual pleasure. Sperm are received into the vagina which is also the birth canal and urine is eliminated from the female body through the urethra.

The female body undergoes many glorious changes every month in the form of the menstrual cycle to prepare for the production of life. Each month like clockwork, hormones are released from the brain which set off a chain reaction

L♥ve N♥tes F♥r Y♥ur B♥dy

_____

_____

_____

_____

_____

_____

_____

_____

_____

_____

_____

_____

_____

_____

_____

_____

_____

_____

_____

_____

_____

of events that alerts the female body for conception. Once the signal is given that conception did not occur, the body goes through another chain of events to reverse these preparations and return the body to its original state. Each month, a woman goes through these physical and hormonal changes from the time she is 12 to approximately 45 years old.

Once the child-bearing years have passed, a woman's body goes through another glorious change called menopause. Menopause is the time when the body begins to shut off/shut down the monthly hormonal surges and changes. This stage is called menopause because it is a pause or cessation of the monthly menstrual cycle.

To discuss and document the glory, wonder and beauty of the female body before, during and after pregnancy would require multiple volumes. I experienced this wonder firsthand during the birth of my third son, Daniel. To this day, it amazes me that during the most beautiful stage in a woman's life (pregnancy), a woman thinks she's fat and unattractive. This is a lie from the pit of hell. Unfortunately, too many women believe this is true.

Because the female body is so specialized and most of the sexual reproductive organs are located within her body, much precaution and care must be taken through regular check-ups. These examinations should be done by each woman on a monthly basis and by your gynecologist annually.

GENITAL SELF-EXAMINATION (GSE)

A self-examination of your genitals should be a regular part of every woman's monthly home health care. This self-exam is important because it may help you discover signs or symptoms of a gynecological problem. Additionally, you will learn about and appreciate the intimate parts of your body.

An added advantage to doing your own monthly **GSE** is that you become more acquainted with these parts of your body. Consequently, you will not just accept what a doctor says without questioning his diagnosis or at least ask for a second opinion. Keep in mind, however, that the genital self-exam is not designed to be a replacement for the pelvic exam and pap smear that your doctor performs. I highly recommend every woman to have an annual pelvic exam and pap smear done by her physician.

L♥ve N♥tes F♥r Y♥ur B♥dy

_____

_____

_____

_____

_____

_____

_____

_____

_____

_____

_____

_____

_____

_____

_____

_____

_____

_____

HOW TO GIVE YOURSELF A GENITAL SELF-EXAMINATION

Before attempting this procedure, you will need:

- ♥ A mirror

- ♥ A lamp

- ♥ K-Y Jelly

- ♥ A plastic speculum (This item can be purchased from a medical supply distributor for approximately .50 cents each).

Find a comfortable position on your bed or the floor. Sit, squat or kneel and prop several pillows behind your back. Bend your knees and spread your legs wide apart. Position the mirror so you can see your external genitals. Shine the light on the mirror. The reflection will allow you to see the entire area more clearly.

THE EXTERNAL SELF-EXAM

1. Start by spreading your pubic hair apart with your fingers. The hairs may be coarse and curly. In older women, the hair may be sparse and thinner. Check for bumps, sores, blisters and genital warts. These may appear as bumpy spots or small growths.

2. Next, spread your outer vaginal lips or the labia majora. These folds of fatty tissue protect the vaginal and urinary area. The inside of these lips are smooth and dotted with small bumps. Don't worry, the small bumps are oil glands which keep the area moist. This area should be light pink to brownish black in color.

3. You will notice two long folds of skin inside the outer lips. These are the inner vaginal lips or the labia minora. They are hairless, very sensitive, light pink or brownish black in color and may be smooth or wrinkled. They usually protrude less than the outer lips. The upper portion of the lips comes together in a hood and covers your clitoris. Below the clitoris is the urethral meatus where urine is passed from the body. As you move down from the urethral meatus, you will see the vaginal opening. Your vagina will appear as two folds of flesh.

THE INTERNAL SELF-EXAM

1. Lubricate your speculum with K-Y Jelly. Do not use too much.

2. Insert the speculum into your vagina with the blades turned downward toward the floor. Insert the blades all the way in, then rotate the speculum

L♥ve N♥tes F♥r Y♥ur B♥dy

_____

_____

_____

_____

_____

_____

_____

_____

_____

_____

_____

_____

_____

_____

_____

_____

_____

_____

_____

_____

_____

_____

_____

_____

_____

so the handle points up.

3. Now grasp the handle and pull the shorter section toward you. Push the outside section down until you hear a click. Your speculum is now locked open.

4. Using the mirror and light, look for your cervix. It may appear like a shiny knob with a dent, hole or slit in it. The color of your cervix may vary from pink to light blue. If you are pregnant, it will be bluish in color. If you are older, it will be pale pink in color. You may notice a discharge coming from the opening in your cervix. This opening is called the os. This discharge is normal and may be clear to milky white in color and watery to creamy in consistency.

5. You may notice some small fluid-filled cysts on your cervix. These are called Nabothian cysts. They are nothing to worry about.

6. Feel your vaginal walls and cervix with your fingers for bumps, lumps or rough areas. If you notice anything abnormal, see your doctor.

7. Remove the speculum. You may remove it while it is still open or close it before you remove it.

8. Clean the speculum thoroughly with rubbing alcohol or an antiseptic soap. Let it dry and place it in a plastic bag for future use.

WHAT TO EXPECT DURING YOUR DOCTOR'S EXAM

There are four basic procedures to a pelvic examination.

1. The External Genital Exam - Your doctor will inspect the vagina and the folds of skin surrounding the vaginal area. This is done to check for redness, irritation, cysts or unusual discharges.

2. The Speculum Exam - A speculum is a metal instrument that is inserted into the vagina to open and separate the walls of the vagina. When the speculum is in place, the doctor checks for growths and abnormal discharges from the cervix. The doctor will insert a small spatula inside your vagina to gently scrape and collect cells from the cervix. This is sent to the laboratory for further microscopic examination. This test detects cancerous cell changes, herpes, yeast and other infections. As your doctor removes the speculum, he will check for irritation and injury to the vaginal wall.

3. The Bimanual Exam - During this exam, your doctor will use both hands. With one hand, he will insert one or two fingers into your vagina. He will

L♥ve N♥tes F♥r Y♥ur B♥dy

_____

_____

_____

_____

_____

_____

_____

_____

_____

_____

_____

_____

_____

_____

_____

_____

_____

_____

_____

_____

_____

use the other hand to press down on your abdomen. This is done to feel your internal organs and check for tenderness, pain, abnormal growths, swollen Fallopian tubes, enlarged ovaries, cysts, tumors and preliminary indications of pregnancy.

4. The Rectovaginal Exam - During this exam, the doctor will remove his fingers from your vagina and insert them into your rectum. This is done to check for tumors behind the uterus, in the rectum and on the lower walls of the vagina. The doctor will also check the condition of the muscles that separate the vagina and the rectum.

BREAST SELF-EXAMINATION (BSE)

(Taken from the pamphlet, How To Do Breast Self-Examination by the American Cancer Society).

There are many good reasons to do a Breast Self-Examination (**BSE**) each month. The best reason is that breast cancer is very curable and easily treated when it is detected early. Another reason is that your understanding, skill and confidence will increase when doing the exam. When you know how your breasts normally feel, you will quickly notice any changes that occur.

The best time to do a BSE is one week after your period when your breasts are not swollen or tender. If you have irregular periods or sometimes skip a month, do a BSE the same day of every month.

HOW TO DO A BREAST SELF-EXAMINATION

1. Lie down and place a pillow under your right shoulder. Position your right arm behind your head.

2. Use the finger pads (the top third of each finger) of your three middle fingers on your left hand to feel your breast for lumps or thickening.

3. Press firm enough so you know how your breast feels. If you are not sure how hard to press, ask your health care provider. Or, copy the way your health care provider uses his finger pads during the breast exam. Learn what your breast feels like most of the time. A firm ridge in the lower curve of each breast is normal.

4. Move around the breast in a set way. You can choose either the circle, the up and down or the wedge method. Do the BSE the same way every time. Make sure you examine the entire breast area and remember how your breast feels each month.

5. Examine your left breast using the right-hand finger pads.

L♥ve N♥tes F♥r Y♥ur B♥dy

_____

_____

_____

_____

_____

_____

_____

_____

_____

_____

_____

_____

_____

_____

_____

_____

_____

_____

_____

_____

_____

6. Repeat steps one through five every month.

7. If you find any changes, see your doctor right away.

You may want to check your breasts while standing in front of a mirror after your BSE each month. See if there are any changes in how your breasts look such as dimpling of the skin, changes in the nipple, redness or swelling. You may also want to do an extra BSE in the shower. Your soapy hands will glide over the wet skin and make it easy to check how your breasts feel.

When you become more familiar with your body, you will get to know yourself. Home self-exams will remove the mystery of your genitals and help you feel more comfortable about your sexuality. In addition, you will detect potential problems at an early stage to seek treatment and a cure. Learn your body and listen to it. It will tell you if something is wrong.

FEMININE HYGIENE AND PERSONAL CARE

Many women have been misled about the delicate subject of feminine hygiene and personal care. Many women feel they shouldn't have any genital odor at all. So, they spend a lot of time and money trying to get rid of "the smell down there." Some genital odor is normal and very erotic to most husbands. If you are experiencing strong offensive odor, the first thing you need to do is examine your personal hygiene practices.

God designed the vagina to continually clean itself by secreting fluids. These fluids are normally odorless. But, if these fluids collect within the vulva area, bacteria will accumulate. If this area is not eventually cleaned, this bacteria will produce a foul odor. Also, dried urine may collect on your pubic hair which adds to this odor.

To eliminate this problem, daily washing is necessary. You should bathe or shower at least once a day. Use mild soap with fairly hot water and bathe the entire vulva area. Separate the vaginal lips and wash between the folds and creases. I advise women to bathe the vulva area in the morning and in the evening. Also, bathing this area is highly recommended after sexual intercourse. If you follow this procedure and still have a strong, objectionable genital odor, you need to visit a doctor. You probably have an infection.

Let me reiterate that your vagina is designed to clean itself. The practice of regular douching can add to your problems because it creates an environment that is conducive to infection. You may be asking yourself, "What is douching?" Douching is the practice of squirting a mixture of water and commercial solutions into the vagina to clean it. A majority of doctors agree that douching should not be done on a regular basis as part of your personal hygiene program.

L♥ve N♥tes F♥r Y♥ur B♥dy

_____
_____
_____
_____
_____
_____
_____
_____
_____
_____
_____
_____
_____
_____
_____
_____
_____
_____
_____
_____
_____
_____
_____
_____
_____
_____
_____
_____
_____
_____

Bacteria exists within your vagina which helps maintain a natural defense against infections. By douching two or three times a week, you wash out the bacteria and weaken your natural defenses. This can and often leads to vaginal infections.

Feminine hygiene sprays, powders and suppositories only bring temporary relief. The fact of the matter is they don't cure the problem, they only cover it up! These products can produce the same problem as douching. Feminine hygiene sprays and powders are forms of perfume that evaporate and leave large amounts of irritants on the skin. All too often, these products aggravate the vulva area and cause allergic reactions. Like douching, feminine hygiene suppositories can change the natural balance of the vagina and cause it to become a breeding ground for bacteria and infections.

There is another area of your body that must be included in the daily care of your personal hygiene. This is the anus and the rectum. Because the anus is closely positioned near the vagina, special care should be given to keep this area as clean as possible. Also, because of the presence of waste material, your anus is always dirty. Regardless of how well you clean this area after a bowel movement, some waste still remains in the rectal area. This waste can eventually cause infections or hemorrhoids.

To clean the rectum, use a thin, square layer of sterilized cotton. Wrap the cotton around your index finger and dip it into lukewarm water. Do not use deodorant soap! Get into a squatting position. Insert your wrapped finger into your rectum and rotate your finger. Repeat this process two or three times until the cotton pad is virtually unsoiled. Clean the outside of the anus using a moistened cotton ball and dry it with toilet paper. This procedure can help prevent the spreading of infections from the rectum to the vagina.

As a woman, you need to love your unique feminine physique and all of its glory. Each stage of a woman's life is marked by beautiful physical changes that are distinct and unique to her species. These changes should be relished and appreciated, not feared and despised.

L♥ve N♥tes F♥r Y♥ur B♥dy

_____

_____

_____

_____

_____

_____

_____

_____

_____

_____

_____

_____

_____

_____

_____

_____

_____

_____

_____

_____

_____

_____

_____

L♥ve N♥tes F♥r Y♥ur B♥dy

UNIQUE AFFIRMATIONS

Below you will find mystique techniques for your unique physique. Renew your mind about your body by repeating and believing these affirmations.

My body is unique.
My flesh is unique.
My skin is unique.
My hair is unique.
My face is unique.
My eyes are unique.
My nose is unique.
My ears are unique.
My lips are unique.
My cheeks are unique.
My neck is unique.
My shoulders are unique.
My arms are unique.
My elbows are unique.
My hands are unique.
My fingers are unique.
My nails are unique.
My breasts are unique.
My nipples are unique.
My stomach is unique.

My navel is unique.
My pelvis is unique.
My pubic hair is unique.
My mound is unique.
My genitals are unique.
My vagina is unique.
My labia are unique.
My clitoris is unique.
My back is unique.
My buttocks are unique.
My hips are unique.
My thighs are unique.
My legs are unique.
My knees are unique.
My calves are unique.
My ankles are unique.
My feet are unique.
My toes are unique.

I am unique!

L♥ve N♥tes F♥r Y♥ur B♥dy

_____

_____

_____

_____

_____

_____

_____

_____

_____

_____

_____

_____

_____

_____

_____

_____

_____

_____

_____

_____

_____

PURRRFECT BODY AFFIRMATIONS

Repeat after me. I am fearfully, wonderfully and purrrfectly made! From my head to my toes, my hair to my feet, I am total female purrrrrfection! Repeat these confessions for a purrrfect body image (just like a kitten—soft, cuddly, tender, sweet, delicate, feminine, graceful, affectionate, etc.)

My spirit is purrrfect.
My heart is purrrfect.
My soul is purrrfect.
My mind is purrrfect.
My body is purrrfect.
My flesh is purrrfect.
My skin is purrrfect.
My hair is purrrfect.
My face is purrrfect.
My eyes are purrrfect.
My nose is purrrfect.
My ears are purrrfect.
My lips are purrrfect.
My cheeks are purrrfect.
My neck is purrrfect.
My shoulders are purrrfect.
My arms are purrrfect.
My elbows are purrrfect.
My hands are purrrfect.
My fingers are purrrfect.
My nails are purrrfect.

My breasts are purrrfect.
My nipples are purrrfect.
My stomach is purrrfect.
My navel is purrrfect.
My pelvis is purrrfect.
My pubic hair is purrrfect.
My mound is purrrfect.
My genitals are purrrfect.
My vagina is purrrfect.
My labia are purrrfect.
My clitoris is purrrfect.
My back is purrrfect.
My buttocks are purrrfect.
My hips are purrrfect.
My thighs are purrrfect.
My legs are purrrfect.
My knees are purrrfect.
My calves are purrrfect.
My ankles are purrrfect.
My feet are purrrfect.
My toes are purrrfect.

L♥ve N♥tes F♥r Y♥ur B♥dy

_____

_____

_____

_____

_____

_____

_____

_____

_____

_____

_____

_____

_____

_____

_____

_____

_____

_____

_____

_____

_____

I am purrrfect!

I am the purrrfect woman!
I am the purrrfect wife!
I am the purrrfect mother!
I am the purrrfect lady!
I am the purrrfect female!
I am the purrrfect friend!
I am the purrrfect lover!

I am absolute purrrrrfection!

L♥ve N♥tes F♥r Y♥ur B♥dy

_____

_____

_____

_____

_____

_____

_____

_____

_____

_____

_____

_____

_____

_____

_____

_____

_____

_____

_____

_____

CHAPTER FIVE

GUYKNEECOLOGY: A MALE GUIDE TO THE FEMALE INSIDE

"A basic course in Guykneecology will provide everything a guy needs to know about a girl—what turns her on and makes her toenails curl!"

CHAPTER FIVE

GUYKNEECOLOGY: A MALE
GUIDE TO THE FEMALE INSIDE

I believe that every husband should be an expert regarding his wife's body. Every husband needs to have a 'B.S.' degree in "Guykneecology," the study and guide to the female inside. Also, every husband needs to be a "guykneecologist," a male sex specialist and authority on the female anatomy.

Most husbands are left in the dark concerning their wife's sexuality because of their own ignorance. Many husbands don't know how to arouse and satisfy their wife sexually. And many wives are too embarrassed or uneducated themselves to teach their husbands what to do and what not to do. This is why too many husbands act like "Mickie the quickie," and their wives are shaking, quaking and faking pleasure and orgasm during lovemaking.

Because of their ignorance of the basic female anatomy, most husbands have certain preconceived notions about sex with their wife. Too many husbands believe the following myths: (1) a wife needs hard, deep penile thrusting to bring her to orgasm; (2) the same things that turn men on sexually excite their wife as well; (3) a wife doesn't need prolonged clitoral stimulation to achieve orgasm; and (4) the bigger their penis is, the more pleasure it will give their wife. Wrong, wrong, wrong and wrong! Wrong on all accounts.

All of these myths and false ideas can be erased with a basic course in Guykneecology. Wives, you can become your husband's female tutor, teacher, trainer, instructor and educator regarding sex and your body. A basic course in Guykneecology will provide everything a guy needs to know about a girl—what turns her on and makes her toenails curl! Wives, become your husband's **W.O.W.** instructor: his **W**ide **O**pen **W**oman and **W**ild **O**rgasmic **W**ife.

I know this concept is new and foreign to many wives. The idea of opening your legs wide and allowing your husband to look at, examine and thoroughly inspect your genitals with the lights on is enough to cause cardiac arrest! There are some husbands who have been married to their wives for 10 to 30 years and still don't know what their wife's vagina looks like. They may know where it is and what it feels like, but not what it looks like. Many married men have to grope in the dark or keep their eyes shut during lovemaking.

It is ironic that this same wife religiously visits the other man—her gynecologist—once a year and allows him to look at her entire vaginal area as long as he pleases. This wife prepares for her visit to the other man better than she pre-

L♥ve N♥tes F♥r Y♥ur B♥dy

_____

_____

_____

_____

_____

_____

_____

_____

_____

_____

_____

_____

_____

_____

_____

_____

_____

_____

_____

_____

_____

pares for lovemaking with her own husband. She takes a bath and a douche. She powders and perfumes her entire body everywhere. She wears her best panties and bra. She purposely leaves early for her appointment because she doesn't want to keep the other man waiting. Once she arrives, she patiently sits and waits to be called. When it's her turn (this man has many women waiting to see him), she walks into the appointed room and without urging, pleading or begging (what her husband usually does to get her to cooperate), she undresses, lays on his table and opens her legs as wide as she can in anticipation for the arrival of the other man. The worst part about it is that he's not even in the room yet!

When he finally arrives an hour later, without romancing, coaxing or even talking, he puts on his gloves, sits on a little stool between her legs and turns on a light above his head. Then, he looks at and touches anything and everything that he wants to! He probes her insides and her outsides. All the while, she never complains, says an unkind word or asks any questions. In her mind, the procedure is necessary and perfectly acceptable. To top this off, after he finishes, this woman pulls up her panties, puts on her pantyhose, says "Thank you" and pays the other man with her husband's money!

Can you see the absurdity of this situation? A woman will open her legs wide to a man she only visits once a year and feels totally comfortable exposing herself to this stranger who may not even know her name. And this man is paid good money to look at her nakedness! Yet, when this woman is at home, her husband (the man who loves her, lives with her and provides for her) is denied the pleasure of seeing her unclothed. Wives, something is seriously wrong with this picture! How can a woman be so comfortable with a virtual stranger, but have inhibitions and hang-ups with her lifelong companion?

Wives in America and around the world must begin to home school their husbands in **"Guykneecology."** The curriculum should include basic courses in **Womanology** (the study of woman, man's glory and sex); **Clitorology** (the scientific study of the clitoris); **Uterology** (the scientific study of the uterus); and **Orgasmology** (the scientific study of the female orgasm).

The course for this study should include the following topics:

- ♥ Female Education - on genitals, sex and the reproductive organs.

- ♥ Female Explanation - on sexual pleasure, arousal, excitement and orgasm.

- ♥ Female Emancipation - freedom to be naked and enjoy sexual pleasure and activities.

- ♥ Female Examination - learning the female genitals by firsthand examination.

L♥ve N♥tes F♥r Y♥ur B♥dy

♥ Female Exploration - discovering the wonders of the female body.

♥ Female Excitation - the art of nipple, clitoral and vaginal stimulation.

♥ Female Exhilaration - includes passion, excitement, climax and orgasm.

♥ Female Elimination - of waste from the bladder, urethra and vaginal area.

♥ Female Evacuation - of waste from the intestines, colon, rectum and anus.

♥ Female Ejaculation - secretion of the fluids and liquids necessary for lubrication before and during sexual intercourse.

♥ Female Exhortation - teaching husbands to cut fingernails (to avoid scratching tender vaginal tissue), and to wash hands and genitals before sex so his affection doesn't lead to infection (the spreading of germs and disease).

KNOWLEDGE IS PLEASURE

Wives, there is another good reason to allow your husband to learn about your body. This reason stems from the basic difference between men and women (husbands and wives) in general.

Men are primarily visual creatures. Women generally rely upon the sense of touch. Men get aroused by what they see. Women are aroused by what they feel. A man can get sexually excited simply by seeing a woman's naked body. But, a woman gets aroused when she is touched, caressed and petted. To a husband, the sight of his wife's genitals arouse him. A wife cannot relate to this because the sight of his genitals does nothing for her unless it is coupled with his caresses. Because of this notable difference, a wife doesn't understand her husband's fascination with seeing, touching and exploring her genitals.

To a husband, the exploration and knowledge of his wife's genitals gives him great pleasure and arousal. Understand that a man has to <u>see</u> something to <u>feel</u> something in order to <u>do</u> something (perform sexually). This is the reason a husband can come home from work, not speak to his wife, be totally engrossed in television all night and prepare for bed. In the process, he catches a glimpse of his wife changing into her nightgown and is instantly aroused and ready for sex. His wife, who has been ignored all evening, is offended, caught off guard and cannot respond appropriately. The husband and wife are at an impasse. The situation is not resolved. So, they turn off the lights and go to sleep frustrated, confused and angry. To him, she's frigid. To her, he's a dog. Both are wrong.

Recently, I was told of an incident between a husband and wife that clearly demonstrates this basic difference. The wife was taken ill and unable to care for

L♥ve N♥tes F♥r Y♥ur B♥dy

_____

_____

_____

_____

_____

_____

_____

_____

_____

_____

_____

_____

_____

_____

_____

_____

_____

_____

_____

_____

_____

her basic sanitary needs. Her illness was feminine in nature which caused her to bleed internally and have a vaginal discharge. Due to these circumstances, her husband had to give her a very intimate cleansing. As she laid there helpless and embarrassed because her husband had to bathe her, she was amazed to find out that her husband was sexually aroused and wanted to make love to her. It blew her mind!

Wives, regardless of how you feel about your body, your husband perceives it differently. He wants to see your body naked with all of its flaws and imperfections. Regardless what you think, your naked body is a turn-on to your husband.

SCHOOL IS OPEN (WIDE OPEN)

Plan a genital examination with your husband. Let me warn you. Although it may begin as an examination, it may end in sexual intercourse. To begin the exam, refer to Chapter 3 of this handbook. Go to the section on "How To Give Yourself A Genital Self-Exam." Make sure you have all of the items listed. Follow the instructions for position and comfort. Allow your husband to thoroughly examine your vaginal area. Let him touch you where he wants, when he wants and as often as he wants. Answer any and all questions he may have. School is open. It's time to learn.

Use this opportunity to show your husband how you like to be touched, caressed and massaged. Show him where your clitoris is located. Guide his hands and teach him how to stimulate you and what feels best. Don't be ashamed to relax and enjoy the sensations you will experience. Let your husband see and feel the delicate tissue of the external and internal vaginal lips. Explain why he needs to be tender when touching you in this area. Allow him to explore your vagina while you share and explain the type of penile thrusting you enjoy most. If this begins to turn both of you on, don't fight the feeling. Finish the class early—it's play time!

Let your husband become your "guykneecologist" and receive pleasure from the examination. I guarantee that your husband will be your best and only student. More than likely, he'll want to stay after school, do extra homework and take many refresher courses. He'll graduate magna cum laude or top of the class!

L♥ve N♥tes F♥r Y♥ur B♥dy

CHAPTER SIX

SEXHERSIZE: WOMAN MOVE YOUR BODY

"Being physically fit is the best gift you can give your body."

CHAPTER SIX

SEXHERSIZE:
WOMAN MOVE YOUR BODY

Of all the nations of the earth, America is the world's leading industrialized nation in terms of military strength and economic power. But, as a people, America is among the worst in terms of physical fitness. The picture gets even worse when you look at the fitness of the entire Christian population!

Most Christians spend a majority of their spare time in church services or doing church-related activities. These activities are usually sedentary (limited physical movement) in nature and revolve around the consumption of high fat, cholesterol, junk foods. In their spare time, most Christians turn into a creature known as the "couch potato."

Christian husbands and wives slouch before the television hour after hour eating snacks and exercising only their fingers on the remote control. For the most part, they don't want to be bothered by anyone. They think their children are hyperactive. But, in reality, their children just want to go outside and play and have fun. The problem is not with the children but with the out of shape, tired and worn out parents.

Although it is not my intention to give a detailed exercise or diet plan, no handbook on the female body would be complete without mentioning exercise and nutrition. Therefore, I will share some basic information for you to consider and act upon. Let me preface this with a precautionary statement. **If you are suffering from a health problem such as diabetes or high blood pressure, I admonish you to consult your doctor for advice before changing your diet or starting an exercise program.**

MOVE YOUR BODY

Being physically fit is the best gift you can give your body. Studies and surveys show that being physically fit has many bonuses. In addition to making you feel great, physical fitness boosts your self-confidence and improves your sex life. People who exercise are generally more interested in sex and engage in the act more frequently. Women who exercise feel more sensual, sexual and in tune with their body. Not only have they gained more respect for their physique, but they also "listen" to their body more.

Although these women do not have a perfect body, they are self-confident and love their body. No one can escape the fact that exercise is vital to your exis-

L♥ve N♥tes F♥r Y♥ur B♥dy

_____

_____

_____

_____

_____

_____

_____

_____

_____

_____

_____

_____

_____

_____

_____

_____

_____

_____

_____

_____

_____

_____

_____

_____

tence and physical well-being. When you are in good physical condition, you perform better in all aspects of life. You work better, live better, love better, play better and rest better. You should look forward to and enjoy your exercise program. I recommend 30 minutes workouts, three to five days per week.

Are you ready? Get set...let's begin to move your body with the following Sexhersizes.

Sexhersize #1

The following exercise will help relieve lower back stiffness and strengthen the muscles in your buttocks, abdomen and pelvic area.

Lie on your back on the floor or a flat surface. Bend your legs toward your chest. Spread your feet apart to the same distance as your hips. With your head resting on the floor, tuck your chin close to your chest and inhale. As you slowly exhale, contract your stomach muscles and press your lower back (the curve beneath your waist) to the floor. Tighten and squeeze your buttocks. Hold this position for five to eight seconds. Relax, inhale and return to your original position. Begin with five tilts and work up to 10.

Sexhersize #2

This exercise will tighten your abdominal muscles.

Lie on your back on the floor or a flat surface. Bend your legs toward your chest. Spread your feet apart to the same distance as your hips. Cross your hands over your chest and place your palms down. Inhale, then slowly exhale and contract your abdominal muscles. To do this, raise your head and shoulders off the floor while keeping your lower back on the floor. Hold this position for two to three seconds. Inhale and lower your head and shoulders but don't let them touch the floor. Repeat for eight times and work up to 20.

Sexhersize #3

This exercise will strengthen your lower back and abdominal muscles.

Lie on your back on the floor with your hands behind your head. Spread your knees apart slightly and flex your feet into the air. Press your lower back to the floor. Exhale and tighten your abdominal muscles as you lift your head forward toward your knees. At the same time, move your knees toward your elbows. Hold this position for two to three seconds then return to your original position. Begin with five repetitions and build up to 12.

L♥ve N♥tes F♥r Y♥ur B♥dy

_____

_____

_____

_____

_____

_____

_____

_____

_____

_____

_____

_____

_____

_____

_____

_____

_____

_____

_____

_____

_____

_____

Sexhersize #4

This exercise will strengthen your abdominal and thigh muscles.

Lie on your back on the floor with your hands behind your head. Open your knees slightly, cross your feet at the ankles and lift them off the ground. Inhale and raise your feet up high while slightly bending your knees. As you exhale, tighten your abdominal muscles and bring your chin toward your chest. Your elbows should be close together and near your knees. Hold this position for two to three seconds. Inhale as you slowly lower your feet to the floor. Repeat this exercise four times and increase it to 12.

Sexhersize #5

This exercise will strengthen your abdominal and side muscles.

Assume the same beginning position as Sexhersize #4, but bend your knees. Open your knees wide but keep your feet crossed. Tighten your abdominal muscles, lift your head and tuck your chin. Reach your right elbow to your left knee. Inhale and lower your arm and leg to the floor. Lift your head and reach your left elbow to your right knee. Repeat this procedure four times and work up to 12.

Sexhersize #6

This exercise will strengthen your side and lower back muscles.

After finishing the above exercise, close your knees and uncross your ankles. Stretch your arms out to your sides. Raise them to shoulder level and place your palms down on the floor. Inhale and lift your knees to your chest as close as possible. With your arms and shoulders still on the floor, exhale and roll your knees to the right. Hold this position for five seconds. Return your knees to the center position. Then roll your knees to the left. Repeat this exercise four times on each side and work up to eight.

Sexhersize #7

This exercise will remove stiffness in your upper and lower back.

After you complete the knee rolls, bring both knees to your chest and hold them with your arms. Slowly raise your head to touch your knees, then lower it to the floor. Repeat two times.

L♥ve N♥tes F♥r Y♥ur B♥dy

_____

_____

_____

_____

_____

_____

_____

_____

_____

_____

_____

_____

_____

_____

_____

_____

_____

_____

_____

_____

_____

_____

Sexhersize #8

This exercise will relieve lower back stiffness.

After finishing Sexhersize #7, hold your left knee with both hands. Pull it toward your chest while keeping your knee bent and your right foot on the floor. Hold this position for 20 to 30 seconds. Repeat this exercise on your right leg.

Sexhersize #9

This exercise will remove tension in your back, neck and shoulders.

Lie on your back on the floor. Stretch both feet forward while sliding your hands along the floor. Keep your feet flexed and your arms over your head. Do not arch your back. Inhale and stretch for six to eight seconds. Tighten your buttocks while you exhale and press your back to the floor. Hold for four seconds. Repeat this exercise two times.

Sexhersize #10

THE KEGEL EXERCISE. Although this exercise is mentioned in a previous chapter, it bears repeating as a part of your regular exercise program. The Kegel Exercise will strengthen the pelvic floor muscles which support your bladder and many of your reproductive organs. This exercise can be done anytime, anywhere and as often as you like.

Inhale and relax your abdomen, buttock and thighs. Concentrate on lifting the series of muscles between your pubic bone and tail bone. Exhale as you tighten the muscle and inhale as you release the muscle. Repeat this exercise 12 times and increase it to 25. It should be done four to five times a day.

L♥ve N♥tes F♥r Y♥ur B♥dy

_____

_____

_____

_____

_____

_____

_____

_____

_____

_____

_____

_____

_____

_____

_____

_____

_____

_____

_____

_____

CONDITIONS AND PROBLEMS PREVENTED AND CORRECTED BY THE KEGEL EXERCISE

CONDITION - SYMPTOM - RESULT

BIRTHING

- ♥ **Delivery** - Easier delivery, less damage to the pelvic and surrounding muscles, reduces the need to use forceps during difficult labor.

- ♥ **Episiotomy** - Reduces the need for episiotomy (surgical cut that widens the vagina during delivery).

- ♥ **Postpartum** - Restores tone and encourages rapid recovery of the female pelvic floor muscles, restores the size of the vaginal canal.

- ♥ **Caesarean Section** - Reduces the need for abdominal delivery by widening the pelvic area for a canal birth.

GENERAL

- ♥ **Chronic Back Pain** - Reduces pain in the lower spine.

- ♥ **Chronic Cystitis** - Decreases persistent irritation of the bladder and urinary tract.

- ♥ **Cystocele** - Minimizes the protrusion of the bladder into the vagina.

- ♥ **Incontinence Urge** - Eliminates over frequent urination.

- ♥ **Urinary Stress** - Stops seepage of urine under stress.

- ♥ **Painful Menstruation** - Diminishes monthly pelvic pain, cramps, etc.

- ♥ **Prolapse of Bladder, Uterus or Rectum** - Decreases the sagging and falling of organs into or protruding outside the vagina.

SEXUAL PROBLEMS

- ♥ **Lack of or Difficulty to Orgasm** - Reduces irritability, lack of sleep, emotional upset and pelvic pain due to sexual tension and failure to orgasm.

- ♥ **Painful Intercourse** - Decreases painful penile entry and thrusting.

- ♥ **Vaginismus** - Reduces the inability of the penis to penetrate the vagina.

FIGURE 2.5

L♥ve N♥tes F♥r Y♥ur B♥dy

_____

_____

_____

_____

_____

_____

_____

_____

_____

_____

_____

_____

_____

_____

_____

_____

_____

_____

_____

_____

_____

_____

_____

_____

_____

NUTRITION

There is an old adage which states, "You are what you eat." This is very true. The Bible declares as a man thinks in his heart, so is he. It is equally true "what a man puts into his mouth, so is he." God is not mocked. Whatsoever a man or woman sows into his or her mouth, he/she will reap in his/her body.

The food you eat is the fuel that your body runs on. If you put cheap gas in your car, it will not run as efficiently as high octane. Have you ever tried to save money and use a cheaper gas from a no-name service station? Several miles later, you pull into a supermarket and attempt to turn off your ignition only to realize that your car has developed a mind of its own. The motor experiences engine run-on and will not stop running. You try again and again but you cannot stop the motor. It keeps sputtering, spitting and running. Then you notice a crowd of people staring and grinning. The gig is up and you're the fool. Everyone knows you put cheap gas in your car.

The same thing occurs when we continually feed our bodies unhealthy food products that have little or no nutritional value. Your bad eating habits may not cause an immediate reaction. But, sooner or later, the law of eventuality will catch up with you and telltale signs will appear such as high blood pressure, diabetes, kidney problems, listlessness and a host of other aliments.

I recommend the following basic foods and food groups to be a part of your daily intake.

RECOMMENDED FRUIT JUICES

♥ *grape juice, tomato juice, orange juice, pineapple juice, prune juice, V-8 juice, apple juice*

RECOMMENDED FRUITS

♥ *apples, dates, pears, strawberries, apricots, figs, fresh pineapple, tangerines, avocados, cherries, prunes, watermelon, bananas, grapes, plums, blueberries, oranges, raisins, peaches, cantaloupe, raspberries*

RECOMMENDED VEGETABLES

♥ *asparagus, spinach, celery, rutabagas, cabbage, beets, lettuce, tomatoes, carrots, turnips, peas, parsley, parsnip, beans, watercress, green peppers, sweet potatoes*

L♥ve N♥tes F♥r Y♥ur B♥dy

_____
_____
_____
_____
_____
_____
_____
_____
_____
_____
_____
_____

_____
_____
_____
_____
_____
_____
_____

RECOMMENDED MEATS

Remove the skin and avoid frying these meats.

♥ *fish, chicken, turkey*

FIGURE 2.3

The following list of recommended foods will keep the organs of your body operating at their peak capacity. Check with your doctor before making any changes in your diet.

ORGAN RECOMMENDED FOODS

♥ **Heart** - *wheat germ, blackstrap molasses, brown rice, sunflower seeds, pumpkin seeds, watermelon*

♥ **Lungs** - *garlic, brewers yeast, brown rice, sunflower seeds, pumpkin seeds*

♥ **Diarrhea or Constipation** - *yogurt, raw apples, persimmons, raw tomatoes, sunflower seeds, cabbage seeds*

♥ **Liver** - *wheat germ, sunflower seeds, pumpkin seeds, lecithin*

♥ **Kidneys** - *raw beet juice, asparagus*

♥ **Uterus, Ovaries** - *lemons (for hot flashes)*

♥ **Gums and Joints** - *alfalfa, yogurt, asparagus, blackstrap molasses*

♥ **Nerves** - *wheat germ, soybeans, pecans, brewers yeast*

♥ **Eyes** - *sunflower seeds, carrots, sweet potatoes, watercress, apricots, collard greens, mustard greens, turnip greens, dandelion greens*

As I stated before, if you are presently under medical care or suffering from a disease like diabetes or high blood pressure, check with your doctor before beginning an exercise program or nutrition plan. Once you begin to improve the care of your body, you will notice an obvious change in how you look and feel.

Love Notes For Your Body

_____
_____
_____
_____
_____
_____
_____
_____
_____
_____
_____
_____
_____
_____
_____
_____
_____
_____
_____
_____

CHAPTER SEVEN

THE LOVE DOCTORS

*"God gave you six ways to love
and nurture your body naturally."*

CHAPTER SEVEN

THE LOVE DOCTORS

I once read an article by Jethro Kloss entitled "The Best Six Doctors." His title was somewhat misleading because I expected to read a list of the top human physicians in the nation along with their specialized fields of practice. Instead, Mr. Kloss listed the following "doctors":

Air ♥ *Water* ♥ *Sunshine* ♥ *Exercise* ♥ *Rest* ♥ *Diet*

I agree with Mr. Kloss and his highly recommended physicians. Notwithstanding, I would like to offer my considerations for the six best "doctors" of love:

Air ♥ *Water* ♥ *Light* ♥ *Exercise* ♥ *Massage* ♥ *Lubrication*

God gave you six ways to love and nurture your body naturally. Four specific areas exist on the female body where these six "doctors" are needed on a regular basis. They are your skin, breast, vaginal and rectal areas. These four areas need a constant supply of air, water, light, exercise, blood (massage) and oil (lubrication) to maintain their health, liveliness and strength.

Believe it or not, your skin is the largest organ of the human body. Not only does it cover and protect vital bodily parts, it also eliminates one third of the impurities from the body. Furthermore, skin is the instrument through which the entire body breathes, absorbs oxygen and exhales carbon dioxide.

Dry skin that shows premature aging is a sign of unhealthy skin. Many women try to hide these telltale signs under make-up and clothes, but cosmetics and fashion do not slow down or stop this degenerate process. Once all clothes and make-up are removed, a woman's healthy skin has good color, is soft to the touch and free of blemishes.

If most women were completely honest with themselves, they would admit they think their vaginal area is ugly, unclean and smelly. It is for this reason that most women are confounded why men are so eager to see what they consider the most disgusting part of their body. For the most part, to a wife, her vaginal area is offensive and revolting. For the most part, to a husband, his wife's vaginal area is beautiful and fascinating. This, along with the fact that he doesn't have a vagina, is why your husband is always interested in seeing yours. However, his wife has a very different opinion.

A woman's negative view of her genital area begins in her childhood. While

Love Notes For Your Body

_____

_____

_____

_____

_____

_____

_____

_____

_____

_____

_____

_____

_____

_____

_____

_____

_____

_____

_____

_____

_____

_____

_____

little boys handle their genitals when urinating and compare the size of their penis to their friends, little girls are taught to be extremely careful when wiping their private parts—being cautious not to touch this area with their hands. Afterward, a girl is told to wash her hands thoroughly. This mind-set was reinforced when she became a woman. For manufacturers of feminine hygiene sprays, douches and sanitary materials convinced women that they needed their products to feel "fresh and clean." As a result, the vaginal area became taboo in the minds of most women. Consequently, women touched and cared for this part of their body as little as possible. The vaginal area was off limits and hidden away under layers of clothes and undergarments. This type of neglect fostered all kinds of vaginal infections.

If the vaginal area is considered unclean by most women, touching the rectal area is completely out of the question. Because the vaginal and rectal openings are situated so close together, bacteria and germs are easily spread from one opening to the other.

LET AIR AND LIGHT LOVE YOUR BODY

Two of God's greatest gifts to humanity are sunshine and fresh air. Together, they produce strong, healthy bodies. Both are in great abundance and free to all partakers. When our society moved from agriculture to urbane, the amount of time man spent in the fresh, clean air greatly diminished. As a whole, mankind has paid for it dearly. Although I do not endorse nudist camps or public nudity of any kind, statistics clearly indicate that nudists have healthier bodies than non-nudists. Let me repeat myself. I am not endorsing public nudity. But, I feel that most women do not enjoy fresh air or receive the benefits of light—be it natural (sunshine) or artificial (indoor lights or sun lamps).

The absence of sunshine causes the skin to lose its natural pigment which is displayed as premature aging. If you do not allow your body to enjoy proper ventilation, it can result in a greater sensitivity to temperature changes. This is especially true in the vaginal area, where the lack of air can foster bacteria and infections. In addition, a great danger exists if you cannot breathe correctly or if your body is not receiving a sufficient supply of oxygen. Some common symptoms associated with this problem include sluggish moving blood, slow heart rate, cloudy thoughts, increase in menstrual cramping, poor sexual performance and susceptibility to disease. To overcome these problems, perform the activities described below.

Love Notes For Your Body

_____

_____

_____

_____

_____

_____

_____

_____

_____

_____

_____

_____

_____

_____

_____

_____

_____

_____

_____

_____

_____

_____

_____

_____

ACTIVITY #1

In the privacy of your own bedroom, remove all of your clothing. Make sure your room has proper ventilation and good natural lighting. If your bedroom is not properly lit, you may want to use artificial lighting such as a sun lamp.

- ♥ Lie on your back with your hands on your stomach. Get comfortable.

- ♥ Inhale slowly. Do not raise your shoulders as you inhale. Make sure your stomach rises and swells like a balloon.

- ♥ Exhale slowly. Let your stomach fall back to normal as you release the old, stale air.

Practice this type of breathing for at least five minutes. Afterward, remain unclothed and continue to relax for another 20 minutes. This exercise is especially refreshing if it is done right after a shower or bath.

LET WATER LOVE YOUR BODY

Water is the most abundant nutrient in your entire body. The consumption and circulation of water is essential to your overall well-being. Internally, water serves as a lubricant to your body. It cushions certain internal organs, gives shape to your cells and regulates your body temperature. Externally, water has great medicinal qualities. Water that is applied to the skin increases blood circulation, tones the epidermis and unclogs pores.

Modern medicine has learned the therapeutic abilities of water. For example, hydrotherapy is the external use of water as a treatment and natural cure for many diseases. In addition, hydrotherapy brings boils to a head, carries away toxins and gives the body an overall sense of health, well-being and relaxation.

The benefits of hydrotherapy can be reproduced in the privacy of your own bathroom. Your bathtub can be utilized to bring home the healing qualities of some of the most popular spas in the world.

According to "The Bathtub Spa" in the September 1991 issue of <u>Healthy</u> magazine, taking aerated or carbonated baths eases lower back pain and over-sensitivity to the cold. They are also useful in the relief of minor aches and pains.

Adding herbal oils or salts to your bath has been found to be soothing to your body and mind. Japanese studies show that many aromatic scents, such as camphor, mint and eucalyptus, produce brain-wave patterns that are associated with relaxation. They also open your respiratory passages so you can breathe better and relax more. So, turn your bathtub into a refreshing spa and let your body take full advantage of the benefits of water.

Love Notes For Your Body

_____

_____

_____

_____

_____

_____

_____

_____

_____

_____

_____

_____

_____

_____

_____

_____

_____

_____

_____

_____

_____

_____

_____

_____

FORMS OF HYDROTHERAPY

Hot Baths ♥ The water temperature of a hot bath is between 95°-110° degrees. The hot bath causes deep relaxation, relieves tension in the muscles and slows down your pulse rate. This type of bath brings relief from nervousness and promotes sound sleep.

Cold Baths ♥ The water temperature of a cold bath is between 50°-60° degrees. You should soak in a cold bath for no more than 10 minutes. The cold bath is the most effective form of hydrotherapy. They have been successfully used to treat hemorrhaging, diabetes, cancer, fever, obesity, skin diseases, infections and shock. **WARNING:** Do not take a cold bath if you are overly tired or severely overheated, if you have cardiovascular disease or kidney problems, immediately before or after a meal, or during your menstrual period.

Sitz Baths ♥ A sitz bath is a very shallow bath consisting of four to six inches of water. The sitz bath can be hot or cold. This type of bath remedies menstrual difficulties, vaginal infections and the vaginal area after childbirth when an episiotomy has been done.

ACTIVITY #2

Begin by taking a hot shower. After your body becomes acclimated to the water (about two minutes), slowly change the water temperature to warm until it becomes a cold shower. After two minutes, slowly change the water temperature back to warm until it becomes a hot shower again. Alternate from hot to cold and back again several more times. End this activity with a cold shower. This type of hydrotherapy stimulates your body and helps build up its internal resistance.

LET OIL LOVE YOUR BODY

Oils have the ability to penetrate the outer layer of your skin to an underlying area and make a dramatic, healthy change. In addition, certain essential oils excite the senses and promote sensuality and sexuality. The Bible alludes to this when it mentions anointing the bed and body with myrrh (a sweet-smelling oil) in preparation for lovemaking. Some of the oils that excite the senses are ylang-ylang, rose, sandalwood, jasmine and linden blossom.

Certain oils also help reduce gynecological problems. For example, clary sage is used to diminish menstrual cramps, ylang-ylang reduces PMS tension, juniper decreases water retention, sandalwood lessens bladder cystitis and rose or bergamot reduces yeast infection. When you apply 100% pure oils on your face, do

L♥ve N♥tes F♥r Y♥ur B♥dy

_____

_____

_____

_____

_____

_____

_____

_____

_____

_____

_____

_____

_____

_____

_____

_____

_____

_____

_____

_____

_____

_____

_____

not use them at full strength. These highly concentrated oils must be diluted with other oils such as sunflower, olive, soy, peanut, vegetable or salad oil. Never use mineral oils, such as baby oil, with these oils.

ACTIVITY #3

Choose an oil like jojoba, lavender, rose or myrrh. If you do not have any of these oils, use olive or sunflower oil instead. Anoint your entire body, gently massaging the oil into your skin. Relax for one half hour and allow the oil to penetrate and sooth the skin of your body. This can be done as often as you want, but at least twice a week.

MASSAGE AND YOUR BODY

Your skin plays a very significant part in your physical appeal. More importantly, skin is vital to your health and well-being. Your body is designed to constantly clean itself and remove toxins. The elimination of impurities is the work of your excretory system which consists of your skin, lungs, kidneys, bladder, ureters, urethra, bowels and anus. This may come as a surprise to you, but your skin actually eliminates one third of the impurities of your body. When the pores of your skin become clogged, your other excretory organs work much harder. This puts a strain on them which can weaken and damage these essential organs.

One way to maintain healthy skin and a healthy body is the dry brush massage. A dry brush massage is just what the name implies—massaging your body with a dry brush. The best brush to use has a natural bristle and a long handle so you can reach all of the difficult parts of your body. Do not use a nylon or synthetic fiber brush because they may pierce, puncture and damage your skin. The following are the benefits of a dry brush massage.

- ♥ It will help prevent premature aging.
- ♥ It will increase and improve blood circulation.
- ♥ It will remove surface impurities and layers of dead skin.
- ♥ It will unclog pores.
- ♥ It will improve muscle tone.
- ♥ It will help distribute cellulite and fat deposits.
- ♥ It will stimulate oil and hormone-producing glands.

Love Notes For Your Body

_____

_____

_____

_____

_____

_____

_____

_____

_____

_____

_____

_____

_____

_____

_____

_____

_____

_____

_____

_____

_____

_____

_____

_____

_____

Three general reminders concerning the dry brush massage are: (1) do not brush your face because it is too sensitive; (2) do not brush tender skin or delicate folds; and (3) do not brush any area of your skin that is infected or irritated. If you have dry skin, shower after the massage and apply olive oil, safflower oil, almond oil or sesame oil to your body. Blot off the excessive oil with a dry towel. After a dry brush massage, always remember to wash your brush with soapy water and let it dry naturally.

ACTIVITY #4

Remove your clothes. Using a natural bristle brush, start brushing the soles of your feet using a circular motion. Move to the top of your feet, then to your legs, hands, arms, stomach, chest, back and neck. The entire massage should take approximately 10 minutes. Follow the dry brush massage with a hot or cold shower.

L♥ve N♥tes F♥r Y♥ur B♥dy

_____

_____

_____

_____

_____

_____

_____

_____

_____

_____

_____

_____

_____

_____

_____

_____

_____

_____

_____

_____

_____

I Love My Body!

SISTER JOYCE WILLIAMS

CHAPTER EIGHT

SINGLES, LOVE YOUR BODY NOW AS YOU PREPARE FOR MARRIAGE

By Sister Joyce Williams

"We waste a lot of time worrying about the future, scouting out marital prospects and getting involved in unproductive activities."

CHAPTER EIGHT

SINGLES, LOVE YOUR BODY NOW AS YOU PREPARE FOR MARRIAGE

As a single, Christian female, I have noticed a very negative mind-set among Christian singles—especially ladies. This pattern of thinking fosters depression, low self-esteem, inactivity, competition and the loss of friends.

What mind-set am I referring to? The mind-set that thinks "all I have to do is pray, fast and read my Bible and God will send me a husband." This mind-set has caused much grief and heartache in the lives of single men and women alike. This mind-set believes that a woman doesn't have to do anything to prepare herself for marriage. This mind-set believes that a woman must completely ignore her physical body to be single and holy. This mind-set will deceive you into believing that your husband will love you only for your spirit—not your body. This mind-set believes anything that deals with or relates to the physical is carnal and sinful. However, when this same mind-set sees an eligible brother, is attracted to him and locks in on him, everything shifts from the spiritual to the natural. Prayer and fasting are quickly replaced with plotting and planning how to meet, court and win him. This is carnal!

As single sisters in the Lord, we must love our body now as we ready ourselves spiritually, mentally, emotionally and physically for marriage. I call this period of prenuptial preparation the **"Esther Factor with a Ruth Mentality."** In other words, single women should be working now and simultaneously preparing for later. Unfortunately, this is not the case with most single ladies. We waste a lot of time worrying about the future, scouting out marital prospects and getting involved in unproductive activities. We need to renew our mind and change our outlook during this period.

Let me preface this chapter by saying that I am addressing single ladies (never married, divorced or widowed) who want, plan and hope to get married someday in the future. To those of you who are confirmed career ladies or permanent bachelorettes, I say, "God bless you." This is not my mind-set. Let me clearly state my feelings on this subject: I WANT TO BE MARRIED!

I have become very focused because I know what I want. Notice that I said I am focused—not obsessed. I know what my goal is and have my sights set on achieving it. My sights are set on a goal, not a guy; on a dream, not a dude; and on a vision, not a victim. My attention is focused on a purpose to be achieved, not a person to be attained. And I know that as I delight in the Lord, He will give me the desires of my heart.

Love Notes For Your Body

_____

_____

_____

_____

_____

_____

_____

_____

_____

_____

_____

_____

_____

_____

_____

_____

_____

_____

_____

_____

_____

_____

_____

In Proverbs 18:22, the Bible says, "*Whoso findeth a wife findeth a good thing, and obtaineth favour of the Lord.*" This Scripture informs me that I am to be found. This means I am not supposed to do the looking. Now, I do have the final word in who can claim me after I've been found, but he has to look for me. My job is to prepare myself to be found. For this reason, I prepare myself as a treasure to be discovered by my future husband.

THE RUTH MENTALITY

If you read the biblical story of Ruth, the account paints a picture of despair and documents many reasons to feel hopeless. First of all, Ruth was from the tribe of Moab. Moab was born of the incestuous relationship between Lot and his oldest daughter after they fled from Sodom and Gomorrah (Genesis 19:30-38). Consequently, Ruth's ancestry was cursed and nothing to be proud of.

Despite the history of bad blood between Israel and Moab, Ruth married a Jewish man from Bethlehem-Judah by the name of Chilion. Both Chilion and his brother Mahlon died prematurely. Ruth was instantly widowed and left with her sister-in-law, Orpah and her mother-in-law, Naomi. Three widows were left to fend for themselves in a land with no welfare system or Social Security benefits. With no where else to go, Naomi decided to return to her homeland of Bethlehem-Judah. Orpah, chose to part company and return to her home land. Ruth decided to follow her mother-in-law and go to Bethlehem.

Now, at that time, the Jews hated the Moabites. A Moabite was considered unclean and not allowed to enter the Jewish Temple. But, because of her commitment and love for her mother-in-law, Ruth went to Bethlehem. As soon as they arrived, Ruth looked for work. She found a field to glean and gathered the fallen grains to feed herself and Naomi.

Ruth is so diligent that the other workers take notice of her. Ruth not only attracts their attention, she also catches the eye of the owner of the vineyard. He just happened to be a man named Boaz who was the most eligible bachelor in Bethlehem. Ruth is so busy gleaning the fields she is unaware that this rich bachelor is watching her and asking questions about her. After her hard day's work, Ruth goes home with an abundance of grain. Naomi asks her where she gleaned. Ruth tells her about Boaz and learns that he is the kinsman of her dead husband who has the authority to redeem Chilion's inheritance and marry her. Ruth hit the jackpot!

After some instruction by her mother-in-law on what to do, Ruth became the wife of Boaz. In addition, because Ruth had favor with God and man, her name is listed in the genealogy of King David and Jesus Christ.

L♥ve N♥tes F♥r Y♥ur B♥dy

_____

_____

_____

_____

_____

_____

_____

_____

_____

_____

_____

_____

_____

_____

_____

_____

_____

_____

_____

_____

_____

_____

_____

_____

Ruth had a choice in the matter. Life dealt her a big blow—death to her husband early in their marriage. Rather than having a "pity party," Ruth decided to work hard and provide for Naomi and herself. After all, she was capable. Ruth did not waste time feeling sorry for herself, singing the blues or crying about the terrible misfortune. On the contrary, she put the past behind and went on with her life.

She got up early everyday and went to work. It was through this activity that God supplied His provision. Boaz found his future wife while she was working. As a matter of fact, it was her hard work that caught and held his attention. I believe many other single ladies in Israel were vying for Boaz's attention, but Ruth won him with hard work and faithfulness.

Tell me truthfully, if a Boaz was to come to your church, what would he see you doing? Would he see you busy working in the ministry or busy working your mouth gossiping? Would he find you committed to the vision of the church or find you causing division in the church? Would he find you purely loving your brothers in the Lord or perversely lusting after every man (including the pastor) with ungodly desires?

If you checked the Bible, you would find that all of the great patriarchs in the Old Testament had the same prerequisite for a wife. She had to be a hard worker. If you don't believe me, just read your Bible. You will discover that God's great men looked for women who were active and working.

For example, Isaac's servant asked God to reveal his master's wife as the one who would offer water to his camels. When Rebecca offered the servant drink and proceeded to water the camels as well, he knew this particular woman was chosen by God to be Issac's wife. When Jacob fled to his uncle's house to be protected from his brother Esau, his first encounter with Rachel was at a well. She traveled great distances to water her father's sheep. When King Lemuel's mother instructed him on how to find a proper wife, she told him to look for a hard worker. One who rises early to work and does not eat the bread of idleness. Saints, it's time to have a reality check. Are you a "Ruth-like" single or a "ruthless" single who cuts everyone with your sharp tongue?

THE ESTHER FACTOR

The second part of the formula for the successful single preparing for marriage relates to Esther. Esther was an orphaned, exiled Jewish girl who was raised by her uncle. The two lived in the heathen nation of Persia. The king of that province disposed of the reigning queen because of her insubordination. At a certain time, he decided to look for another queen. Therefore, all of the beauti-

L♥ve N♥tes F♥r Y♥ur B♥dy

_____

_____

_____

_____

_____

_____

_____

_____

_____

_____

_____

_____

_____

_____

_____

_____

_____

_____

_____

_____

_____

ful maidens of that kingdom were rounded up and brought to the palace. Thus, the first beauty contest. Esther was one of the lovely maidens who was highly favored to be the next queen.

Chapter Two of her book records how Esther prepared herself for an entire year before she was presented to the king. She underwent six months of beauty treatments with oil of myrrh and a stringent diet, and six more months of treatments with special perfumes and ointments. Before Esther was formally introduced, she was decorated with jewelry and dressed in special garments which enhanced her natural beauty.

When Esther's time came to be presented to the king, he was so overwhelmed that he immediately made Esther queen. Esther had this mighty king eating out of her hands! He was so taken back by her beauty that he granted her anything—even the half of his kingdom. Surely, the heart of this king was in the hand of the Lord.

As queen, Esther stopped a plot that would have wiped out the entire nation of Israel. She became a heroine to her people and a special holiday was dedicated to memorialize her achievement.

Esther had to compete against hundreds of beautiful maidens to win one king. She didn't compete by gossiping about the other maidens. She didn't compete by belittling their persons. And she didn't compete by demeaning their character. There was no mudslinging in this contest. Esther competed by improving herself and becoming the best she could be. In turn, she became the Queen of Persia and saved the Jewish people.

Reality check time! How are you preparing for marriage? What books have you read on being a godly wife and a natural help meet? When was the last time you sought instruction, guidance and council from an older married sister about how to love your husband? Are you exercising and eating right to prepare your body for marriage and child-bearing? If not, why not?

MY TESTIMONY

The year of 1977 was a turning point in my life. I was engaged to the most wonderful man in the world, when suddenly our relationship was over. My engagement was broken and so was my heart! For the next two years, I tried to cover up my deep hurt by going out dancing and being the life of the party.

I excelled at work and was quickly promoted to a supervisory position. I shopped in chic boutiques and hung out with a group of ladies who were considered the in-crowd (fashion models in the local limelight). But, each night ended the same for me. I went home after the party and cried myself to sleep. I

L♥ve N♥tes F♥r Y♥ur B♥dy

_____

_____

_____

_____

_____

_____

_____

_____

_____

_____

_____

_____

_____

_____

_____

_____

_____

_____

_____

_____

_____

_____

_____

_____

actually believed that my chance for true happiness was gone forever. I thought I would live alone forever and die unloved. On the outside, I appeared to have it all together. But, on the inside, I was empty.

Finally, one February night in 1979, a friend witnessed to me about the love of Jesus. I was receptive and decided to put Christ to the test. I would accept Him if He could help me make it through the night without tears. Well, needless to say, He gave me a night of no tears. The next day, I received Jesus into my heart as my personal Lord and Savior. At that moment, I literally felt a 50-pound weight lift off my shoulders. I was so grateful to be free that I told the Lord I wanted to be a witness for Him. Well...God honored my request and held me to my word. For the last seventeen years, I have lived a celibate life. Yes, that's right...no sex! Not only has there been no sex in my life, but there's been no petting, no fondling, no kissing and no hugging! In other words, NOTHING!

Please realize that I am not abnormal, superhuman, a eunuch or specially anointed to live this way. I am a normal woman with normal feelings, including a healthy sex drive. But, as Apostle Greenup says, since I've not been licensed to drive (marriage), I must control my motor (sex drive). I don't ignore or deny my sex drive—I defy and control it. I bring my body under subjection and present it to God as a living sacrifice.

As Apostle Greenup says in the lyrics to his rap song **"No Wed No Bed"**

I'm a born again Christian,
Haven't you heard,
Get your hands off my body,
Keep your mind on the Word.

I'm not for rent,
I ain't for sale,
So get out of my face,
I ain't going to hell.

I know you want a hug,
I know you want a kiss,
But until we get married,
You won't touch this!

You may be asking yourself, "How have I maintained this attitude?" I have practiced the Esther Factor and the Ruth Mentality my entire Christian life.

A few months after I received Christ, my beloved mother was diagnosed with Alzheimer's disease. I am the youngest of ten children. At the time she was

L♥ve N♥tes F♥r Y♥ur B♥dy

_____

_____

_____

_____

_____

_____

_____

_____

_____

_____

_____

_____

_____

_____

_____

_____

_____

_____

_____

_____

_____

_____

diagnosed, I was the only child still living at home. I was single and had no children. I decided to take care of my mother—no matter what the cost. I cared for my mother for the next eight years. It was during this period that I learned the meaning of the word "sacrifice." Before my mother's illness, I didn't know how to boil water. But, due to her ailment, I learned how to cook, handle a family budget and be responsible for another individual 24 hours a day.

Instead of crying or becoming depressed, I decided to overcome my situation with work. After all, my mother's life and future existence depended on me and my attitude. Consequently, I adopted the Ruth Mentality. I refused to sit down, be passive and give up. I began to work like never before. I learned how to care for my mother and take care of a house.

I also worked in the ministry as a member of the praise and worship team. During this time, the group ministered at every church service and traveled with Apostle Greenup. Whenever there was an activity at church, I volunteered to help. I cleaned toilets and scrubbed floors on my hands and knees. I did just about everything that I could do. During this time, my duties at work didn't lighten up either. I maintained my position as a supervisor, overseeing several programs and many employees.

You may be asking yourself, "How were you able to do all of this?" This is where the Esther Factor comes into play. I changed my mind-set about my circumstances. I realized that I could prepare for marriage as a single. Everything that I did was viewed from the perspective of training for my future marriage. Not once did I think these things were destroying me or a waste of my valuable time. I learned from every situation in my life and used it to prepare me to be a good help meet. My prayer was, "Jesus, how can I use this in marriage to help my future husband?"

At home, as I cared for my mother whom I adored and respected more than words can express, I learned how to be a housewife. My position on the praise team did not just give me an opportunity to minister as a psalmist, it prepared me to be a minister and psalmist with my future husband. (I truly believe he is a fivefold minister). My secular job provided the income that I needed to support my mother and trained me for my current position as the administrator and secretary to Apostle and Sister Karen Greenup. In my honest estimation, Apostle Louis Greenup and his wife Karen are the best bosses in the entire world (they're going to read this—I'm no fool!) Working for the ministry these past five years is preparing me to work with my future husband in his ministry office.

I feel very fortunate and favored by God to have been placed in a position to observe, work with and have access to *"The Marriage Doctor"* and *"Nurse Good*

L♥ve N♥tes F♥r Y♥ur B♥dy

_____

_____

_____

_____

_____

_____

_____

_____

_____

_____

_____

_____

_____

_____

_____

_____

_____

_____

_____

_____

_____

_____

Thing." Let me reassure you, I take full advantage of this position. I borrow books from Apostle Greenup's extensive library on marriage; I receive counsel from Mrs. Greenup on marriage and being a good wife; I've been blessed to help Apostle Greenup with the writing of his books; and I've had the opportunity to partake of their spirit and observe how a marriage can be successful and victorious through dedication and hard work. I know I have a godly prototype for a man and husband in Apostle Greenup and a godly role model for a woman, wife and lover in Sister Karen Greenup.

MY ONE WEAKNESS

There is a part of my testimony that is missing. Before accepting Christ, I was very conscious of my body. I watched over my weight and made sure I stayed within my perfect body weight. I pampered myself and took great care of my looks. At that time, I was also a heavy cigarette smoker averaging over one pack a day.

I stopped smoking soon after I accepted Christ and before I became a member of my present church. With no nicotine to suppress my taste buds, they came to life. Food started to taste good again and I began to eat. Also, I was instructed by a well-meaning sister in Christ that as a godly woman, I was not supposed to wear jewelry, make-up or pants. Since I loved God and wanted to please Him, I tried to live like this.

I thank God that soon thereafter, I learned the truth that holiness does not mean ugliness or drabness. I realized I could wear make-up on my face because God was concerned with the make-up of my heart. I learned I could adorn my outward appearance as long as I adorned the inward part of my being with holy thinking. And I realized that to be concerned with my physical person did not imply I was carnal or guilty of carnality.

As a result, I returned to taking care of the physical Joyce as well as the spiritual Joyce. However, one area of my body was overlooked—my weight. Over the years, food became my best friend. When I was sad, it comforted me. When I was happy, it helped me celebrate. And when I was depressed, it gave me a lift. Food was my all- around crutch. But, unfortunately, over the years, my best friend helped me expand from a size 10 dress to a size 20 dress.

One day, God told me to do a reality check. He asked me, "If I sent you a husband today, that is ready to get married right away, what would you say? Would you answer "yes" to his proposal of marriage? Is there anything else you must do before marriage?" At first, I was ready to shout, "Yes, Lord, bring him now!" Then I stopped and looked at my self. I had to be honest. I answered God's ques-

Love Notes For Your Body

_____

_____

_____

_____

_____

_____

_____

_____

_____

_____

_____

_____

_____

_____

_____

_____

_____

_____

_____

_____

_____

_____

_____

tion and said, "Lord, I would have to ask him to postpone the wedding until I lost some weight."

I'm sure some of you are wondering why in the world I gave that answer. Let me explain. I want to give my husband the best Joyce I can. I want to be in great shape—spiritually, emotionally, physically and financially. I don't just want to be a healthy wife, I want to be a healthy mother as well. I am preparing my body now for my husband.

I want to have what Sister Karen Greenup calls "a nude attitude for my husband and dude." This concept comes from her chapter in Apostle Greenup's book, How to Stop the Other Woman From Stealing Your Husband. When I get married, I want to be like Abishag who danced naked (very scantily clad) before Solomon. I cannot say that I would feel as uninhibited as Abishag if I danced before my husband as a size 20.

I looked at myself in the mirror and inventoried what I wanted or needed to change. The first area I modified was my diet. I changed to low fat eating. I no longer eat a lot of fried foods or sweet desserts. I replaced those foods with vegetables, fruits, chicken, turkey and fish. I also started an exercise program three to four days a week. I have not attained my final goal in dress size, but I am working on it daily. I don't have the body shape I desire, but I'm loving my body into the shape I want it to be.

PUT ON THE GARMENT OF PRAISE

As a single, 44-year-old woman, I could allow myself to get very depressed. If I let myself, I would have the biggest pity-party in the world. In the past, I was incredibly conscious of my body size and shape. Today, I'm the largest size I have ever been. If that's not bad enough, I am 44 years old and still unmarried. Despite these realities, I have learned to appropriate God's Word and put on the garment of praise.

This principle "putting on the garment of praise to lift the spirit of heaviness," has strengthened me during some very difficult times in my life. When the lives of my brother, sister-in-law and nephew were tragically ended by a drunk driver, this principle strengthened me to minister at their funeral. When I arrived home from church and discovered that my mother had died, this principle strengthened me to kneel by her bedside and sing "I Love You Lord." Later, it strengthened me to minister at her funeral. When I ended my engagement to a brother at church, praise enabled me to function each day despite the pain. Today, this principle still strengthens me when I am tempted with loneliness and depression.

L♥ve N♥tes F♥r Y♥ur B♥dy

_____

_____

_____

_____

_____

_____

_____

_____

_____

_____

_____

_____

_____

_____

_____

_____

_____

_____

_____

_____

You are probably wondering what this has to do with loving your body. Everything! Over the years, I have learned an important truth. The spirit of heaviness leads to physical heaviness. Here's how it works. Your human spirit or heart can become weighed down or oppressed by negative thoughts. This heaviness causes emotional heaviness which is expressed as depression, anxiety, worry and fear.

More often than not, when women are depressed or rejected they take comfort in food and eating. Many singles that I know are not gluttons, they are emotional eaters. In my entire life, I have never run into a Christian single at the gym who was working off the spirit of depression on a treadmill. It just doesn't happen. However, I've had many meals with single sisters when the discussion was the woes of being single. One friend in particular used to share the burden of my depressive moments over a 32-ounce Big Gulp and a king size bag of M & M's.

Without a doubt, this kind of emotional heaviness leads to physical heaviness. Physical heaviness eventually leads to obesity. And obesity causes premature death. I would venture to guess that 75-80% of single, Christian women are either overweight or obese. This is what happens. When we look at ourselves in the mirror, we get depressed because of our size. When this occurs, we run to the kitchen and attempt to find comfort in food. This only puts on more weight which makes us feel more depressed. Consequently, we run for more food and the cycle continues over and over again.

Aren't you tired and fed up (excuse the pun) with this vicious cycle? In Proverbs 12:25, the Bible says heaviness in the heart will make you stoop, but a good word will make your heart glad. I have a good word for you. ARISE, AND PUT ON THE GARMENT OF PRAISE!

Regardless if the spirit of heaviness in your life stems from divorce, abuse, rape, rejection, low self-esteem or loneliness, praise can be used to remove the spirit of heaviness and replace it with God's beautiful garment—both inside and outside. In Isaiah 61, it is written that God anointed this prophet to give the nation of Israel beauty for their ashes and the oil of joy for their mourning. As a child of God, you have the opportunity and anointing to make the same exchange. Through praise, you can replace your mourning (bad experiences and memories) with the oil of joy (strength, excitement and newness of life). Praise will also replace your ashes with beauty.

Many single ladies are walking around with some very deep scars and pains they have suffered in past relationships. In the process, friendships have been forfeited and dreams have been shattered. Some single women feel like second-class citizens because they live alone in a couples society. Deep within the recess-

L♥ve N♥tes F♥r Y♥ur B♥dy

_____

_____

_____

_____

_____

_____

_____

_____

_____

_____

_____

_____

_____

_____

_____

_____

_____

_____

_____

_____

_____

es of their beings, some feel they are still single because something is wrong with them. They feel too ugly, too fat, too skinny, too dark or too light to be accepted and loved by a husband. If I have accurately described your inner feelings, you need to replace the spirit of heaviness with the garment of praise.

Christian singles, stop using food as a crutch. Most single activities begin, end or revolve around food and eating. As a result, singles are some of the most out of shape women in the world. Single ladies 30 years old act like they're 50 or 60 years old. We watch a very active world pass us by and comfort ourselves with donuts, cakes, pies and candy. We spend large amounts of our money frequenting fast food restaurants because we don't cook. If you ever want to find out the best places to eat, ask a single lady! She'll have the answer and directions.

Come on, single ladies. It's time to rise up, shake off those sluggish bands and begin to enjoy life. Jesus came into our hearts to give us life more abundantly. Your abundant life doesn't have to wait until you're married. On the contrary, it should begin today! Remove the spirit of heaviness and put on the garment of praise. Begin to praise God for His lovingkindness toward you; praise Him for His love for you; and praise Him for your life.

Refuse to see yourself as anything less than what you are—a child of the King. I've never seen an earthly princess walk with her head down. She understands who she is and so should you. You have royal blood running through your veins. You are the offspring of the King of Kings. Regardless of your body style, size and shape, you are beautiful because God made everyone and everything beautiful.

Learn as a single woman to accept and love your body in its present condition. Realize that it is not something to be beaten down, ignored or denied. Your body is the temple of God and the dwelling place of the Holy Spirit. God created your body—so love and appreciate it. If your body is not in the shape that you desire, love it into shape.

A great way to replace your ashes with beauty and get your body in shape is through "PRAISERCISE." The only equipment you will need is a cassette deck or CD player and your favorite praise tape. Set aside time each day (approximately 30 minutes) to praise the Lord. As you do, simultaneously move your body. As you dance before the Lord, incorporate as many exercises as you know. As you exercise your body, direct all of your attention and praise to the Lord. This is a great way to strengthen your spirit and body at the same time.

BE A SINGLE THAT WINS

Love N♥tes F♥r Y♥ur B♥dy

_____

_____

_____

_____

_____

_____

_____

_____

_____

_____

_____

_____

_____

_____

_____

_____

_____

_____

_____

_____

_____

_____

BE A SINGLE THAT WINS

God wants every single woman to be an overcomer and winner before she gets married. That way, God will join her to another winner in marriage. As single ladies, we should have our life so together and victorious that when a godly man marries us, his life is greatly enhanced. You need to be an addition to your husband—not a subtraction. Our lives should go from great to greater to greatest. As a single woman we should be great; as a woman and a wife we should be greater; and as a woman, wife and mother we should be the "greatest." But, to be the "greatest," you have to start at great.

To get and keep you on the right track, I offer the following principles that have helped me as a single.

- ♥ Live a balanced life of **J.O.Y.** Focus on Jesus first (a holy life); on Others second (a happy life); and then on Yourself (a healthy life). Focus on Jesus by being obedient to His Word and living holy. Focus on others by being a servant. And focus on yourself by enjoying life now as you prepare for marriage.

- ♥ View and use your time as a single to celebrate life and develop your uniqueness. As a single, don't mark the time until you get married. Enjoy your life now. Don't put your life on hold until marriage. If you live your life to the fullest as a single, you will also have a full life as a married woman.

- ♥ Love yourself right now. Don't wait for a man or your husband to love you. Enjoy who you are as a person. Appreciate your gifts and talents. You possess greatness and value, so love yourself now.

- ♥ Take time to pamper yourself and your body. Put the Esther Factor to work in your life. Work out a beauty regimen and stick to it. Every so often, I pamper myself with a long bath scented with my favorite oil. I bathe by candlelight, listen to soft Christian music and sip on a tall glass of sparkling grape juice. Afterward, I anoint my body with lotion and slip into my nicest lingerie. At that point, I feel like a million dollars.

- ♥ Make an attitude adjustment about your body. Regardless of its current size or shape, realize that your body is the residence of the Holy Spirit. God lives within your physical being. Use the love affirmations in this handbook to love your body now. If there are things about your body that you want to improve, do it. Make the desired changes. But, don't criticize your body. Botanists have proven that plants grow and respond better to words of kindness. If a mindless plant is influenced by kind talk, just imagine the effect that kind, loving, encouraging words will have on you.

Love Notes For Your Body

♥ Become a part of the **S.A.M. Club**. S.A.M. is an acronym that means <u>S</u>mile <u>A</u> <u>M</u>ile. The SAM Club is a health program that Apostle Greenup has incorporated for women. As a member of this club, you will begin a health program that emphasizes cardiovascular activities such as walking, jogging and running. These primary exercises are coupled with a positive mental attitude to produce positive results. In the SAM Club, a woman will walk, jog or run with joy and gladness. There is absolutely no murmuring or complaining allowed in this club. You can't wear a frown because that could keep you down!

This program will put pep into your step, a stride in your glide and work your hips and lips as you smile, sing, stride and swing. Walking is the king of exercises. It gives you a total body workout. The SAM Club can also be used while you work in your home or office. Just think of the miles you travel in your home or office during an average day. This program works on your body and your attitude. A smiling face and a steady pace will help you run this race of grace. Singles who smile as they go (walk or push) that extra mile overcome worry, weight and every trial. Walk at your own pace in malls, in your neighborhood or in your living room. You can turn your frown into a smile when you walk, jog or run a mile.

♥ Adopt the Ruth Mentality. Get busy working in the ministry. Let me share a secret with you. Before a man approaches you, he observes your actions and questions others about you. Let your prospective husband find you working like Rebekah, Rachel and Ruth.

♥ Command love and respect from your brothers in the Lord. This is done by the way you carry yourself rather than by the way you dress, walk and talk. Because there is little training on how to attract a prospective husband in a godly way, many single sisters resort to the worldly tactics they learned before they accepted Christ. Unfortunately, these tactics inspire lust not love and make a brother want to take you to bed not the altar.

Be a winning single who lives triumphantly and overcomes daily as you prepare for your future.

L♥ve N♥tes F♥r Y♥ur B♥dy

_____

_____

_____

_____

_____

_____

_____

_____

_____

_____

_____

_____

_____

_____

_____

_____

_____

_____

_____

_____

_____

A DAILY CONFESSION

The Bible says that as a man (or woman) thinks in his (or her) heart, so is he (or she). As a single woman, anchor yourself in the Lord and His provision for your total being—including your spirit, soul, mind and body. With this in mind, I will share how a single woman interprets the 23rd Psalm.

THE 23RD PSALM (A SINGLE LADY'S PRAYER)

Lord, You are my shepherd, my protector, my husband, my lover, my friend and my guide. Therefore, I have no lack. All of my needs—spiritual, emotional and physical—are met by You.

You give me rest in beautiful places and lead me down the paths of peace and serenity.

You give me the strength I need to live righteously as a witness to Your holiness.

Although I may face many obstacles and sometimes the way is dark, I will not be afraid. You are with me every step, guiding and leading me along the way.

Lord, when my enemies rise against me, You act on my behalf and prepare a shield of defense so I am not harmed.

You have anointed me with the oil of gladness; Your blessings abound and overtake me.

I know Your kindness, goodness and faithfulness will always be with me as I walk this path. Later, when I am joined to my husband in marriage, You will continue to be with me all the days of my life, even into eternity.

Thank You, Lord Jesus, my first husband!

L♥ve N♥tes F♥r Y♥ur B♥dy

_____

_____

_____

_____

_____

_____

_____

_____

_____

_____

_____

_____

_____

_____

_____

_____

_____

_____

_____

_____

_____

_____

_____

_____

_____

CHAPTER NINE

HUSBAND, LOVE YOUR WIFE'S BODY TOO!

*"A husband has the power to transform his wife
into a beautiful, self-confident woman by
verbally expressing his love and appreciation for her body."*

CHAPTER NINE

HUSBAND, LOVE YOUR WIFE'S BODY TOO!

I could not end this handbook without admonishing husbands to actively express love for their wife's body. Most husbands don't have a problem lusting after their wife's body. However, these same men need to be encouraged to show love, admiration, appreciation and acceptance for their wife's body.

In Ephesians 5:25, the Bible declares a husband must love his wife as Christ loved the Church. Every husband is commanded to love his wife three ways: (1) spiritually as Christ loved the Church; (2) socially as he loves himself; and (3) sexually as he loves his own body. A husband has the power to transform his wife into a beautiful, self-confident woman by verbally expressing his love and appreciation for her body—how it looks, smells and feels.

Most husbands will read this and say, "How do I get started?" This is the purpose of this chapter. I will show a husband how to verbally express love for his wife's body. The love affirmations listed on the following pages serve as a guide for your husband. If a husband will sincerely and consistently affirm his love for his wife's body using these statements, he will have a new and improved wife in 60 days.

L♥ve N♥tes F♥r Y♥ur B♥dy

BODY AFFIRMATIONS

"I LOVE MY WIFE'S BEAUTIFUL BODY"

Repeat these love affirmations as you talk to your wife and touch her corresponding body parts.

"I love the beauty of your body."

"I love the beauty of your flesh."

"I love the beauty of your skin."

"I love the beauty of your hair."

"I love the beauty of your face."

"I love the beauty of your eyes."

"I love the beauty of your nose."

"I love the beauty of your ears."

"I love the beauty of your lips."

"I love the beauty of your cheeks."

"I love the beauty of your neck."

"I love the beauty of your shoulders."

"I love the beauty of your arms."

"I love the beauty of your elbows."

"I love the beauty of your hands."

"I love the beauty of your fingers."

"I love the beauty of your nails."

"I love the beauty of your breasts."

"I love the beauty of your nipples."

L♥ve N♥tes F♥r Y♥ur B♥dy

_____

_____

_____

_____

_____

_____

_____

_____

_____

_____

_____

_____

_____

_____

_____

_____

_____

_____

_____

_____

_____

_____

_____

_____

_____

_____

_____

"I love the beauty of your stomach."

"I love the beauty of your navel."

"I love the beauty of your pelvis."

"I love the beauty of your pubic hair."

"I love the beauty of your mound."

"I love the beauty of your genitals."

"I love the beauty of your vagina."

"I love the beauty of your labia."

"I love the beauty of your clitoris."

"I love the beauty of your back."

"I love the beauty of your buttocks."

"I love the beauty of your hips."

"I love the beauty of your thighs."

"I love the beauty of your legs."

"I love the beauty of your knees."

"I love the beauty of your calves."

"I love the beauty of your ankles."

"I love the beauty of your feet."

"I love the beauty of your toes."

"I love your beauty!"

Love Notes For Your Body

_____

_____

_____

_____

_____

_____

_____

_____

_____

_____

_____

_____

_____

_____

_____

_____

_____

_____

_____

"My wife is beautiful"

"Your body is beautiful!"

"Your flesh is beautiful!"

"Your skin is beautiful!"

"Your hair is beautiful!"

"Your face is beautiful!"

"Your eyes are beautiful!"

"Your nose is beautiful!"

"Your ears are beautiful!"

"Your lips are beautiful!"

"Your cheeks are beautiful!"

"Your neck is beautiful!"

"Your shoulders are beautiful!"

"Your arms are beautiful!"

"Your elbows are beautiful!"

"Your hands are beautiful!"

"Your fingers are beautiful!"

"Your nails are beautiful!"

"Your breasts are beautiful!"

"Your nipples are beautiful!"

"Your stomach is beautiful!"

"Your navel is beautiful!"

L♥ve N♥tes F♥r Y♥ur B♥dy

_____

_____

_____

_____

_____

_____

_____

_____

_____

_____

_____

_____

_____

_____

_____

_____

_____

_____

_____

_____

_____

_____

"Your pelvis is beautiful!"
"Your pubic hair is beautiful!"
"Your mound is beautiful!"
"Your genitals are beautiful!"
"Your vagina is beautiful!"
"Your labia are beautiful!"
"Your clitoris is beautiful!"
"Your back is beautiful!"
"Your buttocks are beautiful!"
"Your hips are beautiful!"
"Your thighs are beautiful!"
"Your legs are beautiful!"
"Your knees are beautiful!"
"Your calves are beautiful!"
"Your ankles are beautiful!"
"Your feet are beautiful!"
"Your toes are beautiful!"

"You are beautiful!"
"You are gorgeous!"
"You are lovely!"
"You are pretty!"
"You are fine!"

Love Notes For Your Body

_____

_____

_____

_____

_____

_____

_____

_____

_____

_____

_____

_____

_____

_____

_____

_____

_____

_____

_____

_____

_____

_____

_____

_____

(Repeat these affirmations only if they apply)

"You may be big, but you're beautiful!"
"You may be large, but you're lovely!"
"You may be plump, but you're pretty!"
"You may be chubby, but you're cute!"
"You may be fat, but you're fine!"
"You may be huge, but you're horny!"
"You may be skinny, but you're sexy!

Love Notes For Your Body

FROM "A" TO "Z"
WHAT MY WIFE'S BODY MEANS TO ME

Choose an appropriate adjective to describe your wife's body and repeat the following affirmations to her.

<u>Statement (Sample) Your Adjective</u>

Your body is

A - adorable _____

B - beautiful _____

C - cute _____

D - desirable _____

E - electrifying _____

F - fantastic _____

G - gorgeous _____

H - healthy _____

I - ideal _____

J - jewel _____

K - knockout _____

L - lovely _____

M - magnificent _____

N - nice _____

O - orgasmic _____

P - pretty _____

Q - queenly _____

R - romantic _____

S - sensual _____

T - terrific _____

U - unique _____

V - valuable _____

W - wonderful _____

X - x-citing _____

Y - yummy _____

Z - zestful _____

SMILE AND SAY, YESS, I LOVE SEXX!

Affirmations taken from <u>HOW TO STOP THE OTHER WOMAN FROM STEALING YOUR HUSBAND</u> by Apostle Louis Greenup

Make the following revised confessions daily, as often as possible. You will witness a miraculous change in your attitude toward sex and your husband, as you become his sexy spouse.

Yess, I love sexx!

Yess, I love sexx!

Yess, I enjoy sexx!

Yess, I want sexx!

Yess, I need sexx!

Yess, I crave sexx!

Yess, I love sexx in the morning!

Yess, I love sexx at noon!

Yess, I love sexx in the evening!

Yess, I love sexx at night!

I love sexx 24 hours a day!

I love sexx all day and everyday!

I love sexx seven days a week!

I love sexx on Monday!

I love sexx on Tuesday!

I love sexx on Wednesday!

I love sexx on Thursday!

I love sexx on Friday!

I love sexx on Saturday!
I love sexx on Sunday!
I love sexx everyday and every way!
I love sexx in every position, posture, pose and place!
I love sexx standing up, sitting down,
kneeling and lying down!
I love sexx in the bed, in the tub, on the floor,
in the chair and in the kitchen!

I am a woman.
I am a wife.
I am a mother.
I am a lady.
I am sexy.
I am beautiful.
I am lovely.
I am fine.
I am pretty.
I am gorgeous.
I am a sexual person.
I am a sexy woman.
I am a sexy wife.
I am a sexy mother (momma).

I am a sexy lady.

My body is sexy.

My flesh is sexy.

My skin is sexy.

My hair is sexy.

My face is sexy.

My eyes are sexy.

My nose is sexy.

My ears are sexy.

My lips are sexy.

My cheeks are sexy.

My neck is sexy.

My shoulders are sexy.

My arms are sexy.

My elbows are sexy.

My hands are sexy.

My fingers are sexy.

My nails are sexy.

My breasts are sexy.

My nipples are sexy.

My stomach is sexy.

My navel is sexy.

My pelvis is sexy.

My pubic hair is sexy.

My mound is sexy.

My genitals are sexy.

My vagina is sexy.

My labia are sexy.

My clitoris is sexy.

My back is sexy.

My buttocks are sexy.

My hips are sexy.

My thighs are sexy.

My legs are sexy.

My knees are sexy.

My calves are sexy.

My ankles are sexy.

My feet are sexy.

My toes are sexy.

From my head to my feet, I'm hot, sexy and sweet.

I love being a woman.

I love being a wife.

I love being a mother.

I love being a lady.

I love my husband's body, flesh and skin.

I love my husband's penis.

I love my husband's testicles.

I love my husband's touch and caress.
I love my husband's kiss and hug.

TELL YOUR HUSBAND

I love you!
I need you!
I want you!
I hunger for you!
I thirst for you!
I desire you!
I crave you!
I ache for you!
I throb for you!
I long for you!
I yearn for you!
I'm hot for you!
I'm wet for you!
I'm horny for you!
I'm excited about you!
I really enjoy you!

CONCLUSION

Knowing your body is the first step to loving your body. You must learn to overcome any unhealthy image you may have about yourself. At the same time, you must be realistic about who you are and how you look. If you don't love what you see in the mirror, then work to change it—if it can be changed.

Remember, your physical and outward appearance is secondary to the beauty of the Holy Ghost within your spirit being.

Diet, nutrition and exercise are vitally important in your quest for a more beautiful you. As I mentioned before, exercise should be done on a regular and consistent basis.

Once you begin to love and like your body, you will begin to see a "lovelier" you. You should already know you are a UFO—a unique feminine organism unlike any other woman that God has created. From head to toe, you are beautiful, unique and purrrfect.

It's not what you have, what you don't have or even how attractive you are that counts. Rather, it's how you feel and use what you have that really matters. Nothing is more attractive to your husband than a self-confident, self-loving and selfless wife.

Enjoy the new, self-assured and "lovelier" you. Woman...love your body. And let your husband love it too! A healthier, more assured you will impress your mate and improve your marriage. I am living proof of this truth.

Remember, a woman who is free to love herself, is free to love her husband.

APPENDIX

WOMAN, THE BEAUTY OF THE LORD

1 Peter 3:1-6

Amplified Bible

(1) In like manner, you married women, be submissive to your own husbands [subordinate yourselves as being secondary to and dependent on them, and adapt yourselves to them], so that even if any do not obey the Word [of God], they may be won over not by discussion but by the [godly] lives of their wives,

(2) When they observe the pure and modest way in which you conduct yourselves, together with your reverence [for your husband; you are to feel for him all that reverence includes: to respect, defer to, revere him—to honor, esteem, appreciate, prize, and, in the human sense, to adore him, that is, to admire, praise, be devoted to, deeply love and enjoy your husband].

(3) Let not yours be the [merely] external adorning with [elaborate] interweaving and knotting of the hair, the wearing of jewelry, or changes of clothes;

(4) But let it be the inward adorning and beauty of the hidden person of the heart, with the incorruptible and unfading charm of a gentle and peaceful spirit, which [is not anxious or wrought up, but] is very precious in the sight of God.

(5) For it was thus that the pious women of old who hoped in God were [accustomed] to beautify themselves and were submissive to their husbands [adapting themselves to them as themselves secondary and dependent upon them].

(6) It was thus that Sarah obeyed Abraham [following his guidance and acknowledging his headship over her] calling him lord (master, leader, authority). And you are now her true daughters if you do right and let nothing terrify you [not giving way to hysterical fears or letting anxieties unnerve you].

THE GLORY OF THE MAN

1 Corinthians 11:7-9

Amplified Bible

(7) For a man ought not to wear anything on his head [in church], for he is the image and [reflected] glory of God [his function of government reflects the majesty of the divine Rule]; but woman is [the expression of] man's glory [majesty, pre-eminence].

(8) For man was not [created] from woman, but woman from man;

(9) Neither was man created on account of or for the benefit of woman, but woman on account of and for the benefit of man.

A TRULY GOOD WIFE

Proverbs 31:10-31

Living Bible

(10) If you can find a truly good wife, she is worth more than precious gems!

(11) Her husband can trust her, and she will richly satisfy his needs.

(12) She will not hinder him, but help him all her life.

(13) She finds wool and flax and busily spins it.

(14) She buys imported foods, brought by ship from distant ports.

(15) She gets up before dawn to prepare breakfast for her household, and plans the day's work for her servant girls.

(16) She goes out to inspect a field, and buys it; with her own hands she plants a vineyard.

(17) She is energetic, a hard worker,

(18) and watches for bargains. She works far into the night!

(19) She sews for the poor,

(20) and generously helps those in need.

(21) She has no fear of winter for her household, for she has made warm clothes for all of them.

(22) She also upholsters with finest tapestry; her own clothing is beautifully made—a purple gown of pure linen.

(23) Her husband is well known, for he sits in the council chamber with the

other civic leaders.

(24) She makes belted linen garments to sell to the merchants.

(25) She is a woman of strength and dignity, and has no fear of old age.

(26) When she speaks, her words are wise, and kindness is the rule for everything she says.

(27) She watches carefully all that goes on throughout her household, and is never lazy.

(28) Her children stand and bless her; so does her husband. He praises her with these words:

(29) "There are many fine women in the world, but you are the best of them all!"

(30) Charm can be deceptive and beauty doesn't last, but a woman who fears and reverences God shall be greatly praised.

(31) Praise her for the many fine things she does. These good deeds of hers shall bring her honor and recognition from people of importance.

GOD'S IDEAL WOMAN

Proverbs 31:10-31

Amplified Bible

(32) A capable, intelligent, and virtuous woman—who is he who can find her? She is far more precious than jewels and her value is far above rubies or pearls.

(33) The heart of her husband trusts in her confidently and relies on and believes in her securely, so that he has no lack of [honest] gain or need of [dishonest] spoil.

(34) She comforts, encourages, and does him only good as long as there is life within her.

(35) She seeks out wool and flax and works with willing hands [to develop it].

(36) She is like the merchant ships loaded with foodstuffs; she brings her household's food from a far [country].

(37) She rises while yet it is night and gets [spiritual] food for her household and assigns her maids their tasks.

(38) She considers a [new] field before she buys or accepts it [expanding pru-

dently and not courting neglect of her present duties by assuming other duties]; with her savings [of time and strength] she plants fruitful vines in her vineyards.

(39) She girds herself with strength [spiritual, mental, and physical fitness for her God-given task] and makes her arms strong and firm.

(40) She tastes and sees that her gain from work [with and for God] is good; her lamp goes not out, but it burns on continually through the night [of trouble, privation, or sorrow, warning away fear, doubt, and distrust].

(41) She lays her hands to the spindle, and her hands hold the distaff.

(42) She opens her hand to the poor, yes, she reaches out her filled hands to the needy [whether in body, mind, or spirit].

(43) She fears not the snow for her family, for all her household are doubly clothed in scarlet.

(44) She makes for herself coverlets, cushions, and rugs of tapestry. Her clothing is of linen, pure and fine, and of purple [such as that of which the clothing of the priests and the hallowed cloths of the temple were made].

(45) Her husband is known in the [city's] gates, when he sits among the elders of the land.

(46) She makes fine linen garments and leads others to buy them; she delivers to the merchants girdles [or sashes that free one for service].

(47) Strength and dignity are her clothing and her position is strong and secure; she rejoices over the future [the latter day or time to come, knowing that she and her family are in readiness for it]!

(48) She opens her mouth in skillful and godly Wisdom, and on her tongue is the law of kindness [giving counsel and instruction].

(49) She looks well to how things go in her household, and the bread of idleness [gossip, discontent, and self-pity] she will not eat.

(50) Her children rise up and call her blessed (happy, fortunate, and to be envied); and her husband boasts of and praises her, [saying],

(51) Many daughters have done virtuously, nobly, and well [with the strength of character that is steadfast in goodness], but you excel them all.

(52) Charm and grace are deceptive, and beauty is vain [because it is not lasting], but a woman who reverently and worshipfully fears the Lord, she shall be praised!

(53) Give her of the fruit of her hands, and let her own works praise her in the gates [of the city]!

FOUR GOOD REASONS WHY A WOMAN MUST LOVE HER BODY!

1. As a woman, you are essentially a spiritual being who dwells inside a physical body. Therefore, to hate your body is to hate the very essence of who you really are.

2. God lives inside your body which is His fleshly temple. Therefore, to hate your body is to hate the dwelling place of God.

3. Your husband becomes one with you through every act of sexual intercourse. Therefore, to hate your body is to hate God's holy union and the man God has given you.

4. Your body is where your baby grows and develops before he or she enters this world. Therefore, to hate your body is to hate the child God has blessed you with.

HOW TO HANDLE A HUNGRY HUSBAND AT HOME

Feed his need,
Attack his lack,
Wear him out,
But don't hold back.

You don't need soap operas,
You don't need Penthouse,
To teach you how to love,
And satisfy your spouse.

The Bible is the book,
From which we cook,
Just one meal,
And your husband is hooked.

Serve it to him once,
Serve it to him twice,
Add a whole lot of love,
And make it mighty nice.

When you serve it to him hot,
You'll make him beg for more,
When it's time to eat dinner,
He'll knock down your door.

Just ring the dinner bell,
Watch him jump and run,
Fix it real good,
Have a whole lot of fun.

If you want to change your husband,
Take a tip from me,
Come into my kitchen,
And follow my recipe.

This Recipe of Romance is all natural. 100% pure pleasure. No adultery added. No perversion permitted.

RECIPE FOR ROMANCE IN MARRIAGE

For a delectable dish of sensational romance, follow this recipe. The ingredients of intimacy include the following:

1 cup of cuddling
3 teaspoons of teasing
1 dash of desire
2 pinches of passion
1 funnel of fondling
6 grams of gentleness
5 tablespoons of tenderness
3 liters of loving
4 ounces of originality
1 sprinkle of sensation
7 pounds of pleasure

Cooking Instructions:

Faithfully mix all of the ingredients into a great big bowl of blessings. Stir up this gift of God well. If you pour this loving mixture in a pan of plenty, you'll never need an affair. With true commitment of heart (to the Lord and your mate) liberally sprinkle a great deal of attention and affection. Then, turn on your blazing fire of desire to 475° (very hot) and bake slowly for two hours in the oven of obedience until the fulfillment of total intimacy is achieved. What a dish! It's very good.

Mrs. Karen H. Greenup
(a.k.a. *"Nurse Good Thing"*)

WORKS CONSULTED

The American Cancer Society. How To Do Breast Self-Examination.

Cobat, Sandra Dr. The Body-Shaping Diet. New York, New York: Time Warner Co. 1993.

Evans, Debra. The Mystery of Womanhood. Westchester, Illinois: Crossway Books, 1987.

Fletcher, Anne. "Finally Lose Weight! The Self-Esteem Plan." Prevention, January 1991, p. 44.

Jacob, Susan. "The Body Image Blues, Women Reveal Their Secret Fears." Family Circle, February 1990, pp. 41-45.

Kloss, Jethro. "The Best Six Doctors." Natural Health Review, March 1990, pp. 20-22.

Kuriansky, Judy Dr. "Exercise & Sex...Strange Bedfellows." pp. 56-57.

Madaras, Lynda., Patterson, Jane M.D. and Schiek, Peter Dr. Womancare. New York: Avon Books, 1981.

Mitchell, Sandi Dr. "Hydrotherapy." Natural Health Review, March 1990, pp. 20-22.

Morrison, Marsh. "A Doctor Tells You Which Food Is Right for What's Wrong With You." New Woman, September 1984, pp. 73-74, 76-77.

Shafts, Marjorie Dr., Hunt, Gerald L. Every Woman's Guide to the Body at 40. New York, New York: Putnam Publishing Company, 1987.

Sims, Naomi. All About Health & Beauty for the Black Woman. Garden City, New York: Doubleday, 1976.

Stewart, Felicia Dr. Understanding Your Body. New York: Bantam Books, 1987.

"The Bathtub Spa." Healthy, September 1991, p. 2.

"A Breath of Fresh Air." Health Store News, April 1990, p.14.